Papa Mike's
Cook Islands Handbook
Second Edition

MIKE HOLLYWOOD

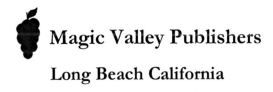
Magic Valley Publishers

Long Beach California

Papa Mike's Cook Islands Handbook
Second Edition

All Rights Reserved © 2008 By Mike Hollywood

Magic Valley Publishers

For information address:

Magic Valley Publishers
6390 E. Willow Street
Long Beach, CA 90815
www.magicvalleypub.com

The author has made every effort to be as accurate as possible, but the passage of time may make some information obsolete. It is always best to confirm information before making plans. The author accepts no liability for any losses that may occur out of using any services provided by businesses listed in this guide. The author would be grateful for both positive and negative comments on any establishment that is recommended in this guide.

Address comments to:

Mike Hollywood
Post Office Box 21
Emigrant, MT 59027

ISBN 978-0-9800879-6-3
Printed in the United States of America

Other Titles By Mike Hollywood

The West Indiies On $50.00 A Day
(Guesthouse Travel In The Caribbean)

Papa Mike's Cook Islands Handbook
(First Edition)

Papa Mike's Palau Islands Handbook

Dedication

Well the last one was for my father and this one is for my kids. I watched Kenny Chesney yesterday, telling everyone that they should not blink, explaining how life goes by so damn fast. I suppose, I second that motion, life has certainly gone by plenty fast for this father. I love those two kids, Matt the guitarist, with a lot of that fiery redhead in his personality, but a lot of Papa Mike to be found in his love of music and creativity. To my daughter Jen, I see so much of me in your every manner and way, you will always be my little miss magic.

In addition I want to dedicate this book to a couple of dear friends that I had the pleasure of knowing in my lifetime. To Phil and Betty Pringle, it was a pleasure to share time with you two. Betty and Phil have been an inspiration to me in my life, the love shared by the two of them have been a constant inspiration to me. I know there is a special place up there in heaven waiting for the two of you.

Contents

Part I The Trip

How to use this Handbook...5

Introduction...7

General
Information..9

Planning Your Trip...25

What To Take...30

Inter Island Transportation...35

Part II The Islands

Rarotonga...46

Aitutaki Atoll...133

Mangaia..164

Manihiki...173

Mauke..179

Mitiaro...188

Penrhyn..198

Atiu..202

Palmerston..215

Suwarrow Atoll...220

Pukapuka...223

Nassau Island...228

Rakahanga..233

Part III Reference

Bibliography..239

About the Author..243

Index

Acknowledgements

So this is the second go around on this book. Some of the same people are to bless and blame for the book. All errors and omissions are very definitely my fault. There are many that helped get the book done, some located south of the equator and some north.

On Rarotonga I relied heavily on that, "cute island girl" Tina, which some of you will remember from the disastrous Northern Island Group hurricane trip aboard the Island Freighter *Manu Nui,* which now lies desirably on the bottom of the South Pacific, scuttled along with the thousands of cockroaches off Rarotonga. Tina, those past Oreo transgressions are well behind us. Thanks for all you do for this old travel writer. Best Island Guacamole maker, best *"Iki Mata"* on Rarotonga, the list goes on and on. All the trips to the airport, many beers and meals, you were always there for me. Most of all thank you for introducing me to Pu and Terry; they are truly the sweetest couple on Rarotonga, now I know where you got all that charm and beauty.

I still smile when I remember departing the arrivals terminal with my fellow Los Angeles passengers, them to their Raro Tours bus and I to a hug a kiss and a lei from the prettiest girl on the island. Lets just say there were a quite a few jealous males in the crowd.

My thanks to Teariki Numanga of Air Rarotonga, thanks for the consideration your company provided me on my outer island trips. A special thank you to Shine at the departure gate, who always saw to it that bulky Papa Mike got one of the front row seats on those small 16-seater Bandeirante planes that make the outer island flights, my knees thank you Shine!

Thanks go out to Jim Bruce and Rondo Perkins, local hotel owners who befriended the author. Both run highly respected lodgings, but much more than that both are truly involved in the preservation of Rarotonga and the Cook Islands.

I have not forgotten the folks that helped me with the original edition of this book; it's just that you received your thanks last time around.

This book would never have been completed without the assistance of many. Listed below is a partial list of many of those that have helped me in my efforts. For those who I fail to mention, I apologize, but I appreciate your efforts, I just can't remember all of your names.

Photography

Angus Gillies, who was kind enough to let me use it, took the wonderful cover shot of the beach on Rarotonga that appears on the front cover. All other photographs were supplied by the author, accommodations or Cook Islands Tourism Board.

Atiu

Roger and Kura Malcomb are shining examples of what can be accomplished with a lot of hard work and a plan. Atiu Villas are a tribute to these two entrepreneurs and that new swimming pool sure is a great addition. Your consideration to a visiting author was greatly appreciated; next time we are off to the *Tumunu,* eh Roger? Thanks to Papa Perere for his great historical tour of the island.

Aitutaki

The second edition allowed me my third visit to the beautiful lagoon of Aitutaki. As always, many islanders helped make my stay enjoyable. Thanks to the people at Tom's Beach Cottage. I enjoyed my little beach cottage on the lagoon. Thanks to John Richards, an ex-patriot with a vast knowledge of Aitutaki. I had a great breakfast, while getting the scoop on changes on the island while I devoured banana pancakes at Koru Café.

Mitiaro

I send my sincere thanks to Vivian Vandongen, her beautiful daughter Mamia Tere Tunoa and her lovely cousin Teverangi Tou. Thanks for sharing your home and meals. It was a special treat for me to share your island, if only for three days. Someday I hope to return and renew the friendship I received from my new "brothers" on the island.

Mauke

It was a wonderful stay on Mauke with Teata and Tangata Ateriano in their lovely little cottage on the reef on Mauke. Wonderful seclusion and the viewing platform on the tip of the reef was a great inspiration for me to expand the whole chapter on Mauke.

Maps

Thanks to John Walters for the use of his island maps. Be sure and visit John's extensive and informative www.ck Website for the oldest and most extensive Website on the Cook Islands.

PART 1

THE TRIP

How to Use This Handbook

Papa Mike's Cook Island Handbook, is your pocket tour guide for the ultimate Cook Islands vacation. It's designed for both the active traveler and the traveler who wants to recline on the same beach for two weeks.

If your goal is to just visit Rarotonga, the book represents the most up to date information on just about every accommodation on the island, from boutique resort hotels to backpacker's lodgings. It describes the wide selection of things to do on Rarotonga and how to go about doing them. The where to eat section will direct you to the author's choices for authentic island food and drinks.

On the other hand if your goal is visit the far off atolls of the outer Cook Islands, the book will tell you how to go about it, what to see, how to get there and how to find accommodations on these far off outposts. Not only will it direct you to the inter-island freighter, it will describe what to take along on the ship and what the shipping line provides in the way of services.

With this handbook you can plan your trip to the Cook Islands from anywhere in the world. The general information section will provide you with entry requirements and practical information on where to obtain the best exchange rates, buy film for your camera, or locate the hospital. In short, the handbook is both a planning tool for a trip to Polynesia and a daily reference for your stay in paradise.

How Much Will It Cost

The major cost of travel to the Cook Islands is the airfare. While part of the beauty of the Cook Islands is the remote location, this beauty has a price tag, as the remoteness leads to very few choices when selecting an airline. Currently there are only two international airlines serving Rarotonga and the Cook Islands. Air New Zealand and Pacific Blue Airlines; check out the, "planning your trip" section of this book for flight information. A reasonably frugal couple traveling from the West Coast of the United States and staying for two weeks, will spend roughly US$2400.00 on coach airfare, US$950.00 for moderate lodging and another US$850.00 for food and miscellaneous items over their stay. By traveling during the off-season, using consolidators, booking budget lodging and cooking some of your own meals the trip can cost as little as US$3000.00 for a couple. As you can see, up to two thirds of the cost of the trip, is the airfare, so it pays to keep an eye on sales and specials offered by consolidators. Check the travel section in your local newspaper for airfare sales and package deals.

You will note that all pricing in the book is given in New Zealand Dollars (NZ$), this is not to favor the Kiwi's but the Cook Island Dollar is interchangeable to and tied in to the value of the New Zealand currency. The American Dollar fluctuates substantially in its value when compared to the New Zealand Dollar. Unrest in the Middle East, interest rates, and the potential for terrorist attacks, can alter the exchange rate of the US dollar. With this in mind, all price references in the book are New Zealand Dollars unless stated otherwise. For current exchange rates, go to the XE Currency Exchange Website, **www.xe.com/ucc/** to use their universal currency converter.

Introduction

It was six years ago almost to the day that I wrote the introduction to the first edition of this book. Over the past six years the Cook Islands have managed to avoid much of the over development that plagues a few of their island neighbors. While overall visitor arrival numbers have increased, the increase is almost exclusively the result of more New Zealander's visiting the islands. Visitor arrivals from the United States and Canada are down over the past six years and while some of the decline can be blamed on the weak dollar, I still find it amazing that more Westerners do not travel beyond the glitz of Hawaii, to a more authentic Polynesian experience. You will still find that the locals are as friendly as ever, the hotels are still mostly small boutique operations and the papayas are always fresh and sweet. The charm remains and as the dollar rebounds it is my hope that more Americans and Canadians will venture beyond Hawaii to this South Pacific paradise.

It has been said that the Cook Islands are what Tahiti was like 50 years ago. I truly think that this is an accurate statement. Lacking a deepwater port, Rarotonga, capital and the most populated island in the Cooks chain, remains much the same as it was thirty to fifty years ago. In some ways this lack of a deep-water port is a blessing, for this lack of berthing has kept those pesky cruise ships away and allowed the islands to avoid rampant tourism and develop slowly. So if you are looking for a pristine group of islands head due south from Honolulu 3000 miles to this tiny chain of islands in the South Pacific, you wont be disappointed.

Tourism is the number one industry on Rarotonga, and the local tourist board has done a fine job in promoting the region. Producing colorful brochures with enough helpful information to the point that one fellow South Pacific guidebook writer limits material on the Cook Islands, specifically because the tourist board prepares such information filled brochures. There is even a free DVD of the islands available from the tourist board. I hope that the islands continue a slow but steady rise in tourism, but that the remoteness of the region continues to shield it from the rampant development that has plagued other island destinations.

Hopefully the islands and the people will remain as they now are and this guide will help you further enjoy your visit to this very special region.

General Information & Facts For The Visitor

As is typical of my guidebooks (all three of them) I will give you mountains of practical information on how to visit the islands. I will not delve into history, geology, flora and fauna, education and the arts in any great detail, as I feel that those that are interested in these subjects will want a much more scholarly rendition than I can offer. Besides I don't enjoy writing about these subjects—so on to practical information.

If you are traveling from the United States, turn left when you get to Hawaii. Well, that really is how you get here and where the Cook Islands are located, 3000 miles south of Hawaii, with Fiji and Samoa to the west and Tahiti and French Polynesia to the east. The climate is very similar to Hawaii and seasons are fairly neutral this close to the equator. There are approximately 15,000 inhabitants of the Cook Islands, with nearly half of those inhabiting Rarotonga, the main island and your arrival point unless you came by paddle, sail or backstroke. The Cook Islanders are primarily of Maori descent, dark skinned and rotund, with flowers in their hair and a broad smile on their faces. They are a kind and friendly people; always anxious to help you enjoy your trip.

Entry Requirements

There are two things you need to have when you arrive in Rarotonga. The first is a valid passport. If you have one, check the expiration date and make sure that when your trip begins, there will be at least six months to the date of expiration. This is a Cook Island requirement and I'll be damned if I know why, but as they say, it is their island, therefore they make the rules and we, as visitors need to comply. If you don't have a passport apply for one and take it with you to the islands. Once you have your passport, make two photocopies of the front identification page. Before you leave give one copy to a relative at home, take the second on your trip and pack it separately from the passport. If you lose or have your passport stolen, you will thank me for taking these steps, as the replacement time is significantly shorter if you have the photocopy. When you arrive in Rarotonga, with your passport, you will automatically be issued a visitor's permit for 31 days.

The second item that you need to gain entry to the country is a hotel reservation. I am not sure if this second requirement was aimed at the sixties hippie movement, but it is a fact of life, and camping is prohibited on the islands. There are many inexpensive accommodations and backpackers have a variety of hostels to chose from. See the accommodation section for specific information. In summer months you can book a couple of nights and then relocate if you are not happy with the establishment. I would not recommend this practice in the busy Christmas Holiday season, as accommodations fill up and you may be without a place to sleep.

Banks & Currency

Well maybe there are more than two things you need when you arrive; I think your trip will be far more enjoyable if you bring some money. The New Zealand dollar is on a par with the Cook Island dollar. The current exchange rate to the American dollar is 1.2 to one, so this makes the local dollar worth US seventy-nine cents. There is a bank at the airport as you arrive, so there is no need to obtain currency prior to arrival. Rarotonga has two banks **Westpac Ph. 22-014** and **ANZ Ph. 21-750**, they are both located in Avarua and offer the similar exchange rates. I found the best exchange rates at **Global Ex Ph. 29-907**, next to Jetsave Travel in the main section of Avarua. Traveler's checks command an additional 4% premium at the banks, for reasons yet to be determined. I recommend you exchange funds in Rarotonga prior to visiting the outer islands; there are no banks on the outer islands and exchange rates may be less than on Rarotonga. Major credit cards are widely accepted on Rarotonga, but less so in the outer islands. The banks in Rarotonga will facilitate cash advances on Visa and MasterCard. Prices are moderate for goods and services. Keep in mind that the islands are remote and most items have to be shipped by boat from New Zealand. There are ATM machines at both banks in Avarua as well as one at the airport and many scattered around in small shops around the island, so you can use a debit or credit card to receive a cash advance. In recent years additional ATM's have been installed at Wigmore's store on Rarotonga and at Mango's Trading on Aitutaki. All ATM's are part of the Cirrus worldwide network, so you should be able to access your home account from the ATM. You will want to talk to your bank prior to leaving on vacation, let them know where you will be and find out about access and fees charged for the service to avoid surprises when you return home.

Electric Service

If you brought your hair dryer, shame on you! Much the same if you brought your electric razor, boom box or portable DVD player. You are supposed to escape all those trappings of civilization when you leave the states. But, if you did bring along or plan to bring along these things you had better bring along a voltage converter for the islands are on 220 volt power system, not our 110 system. Electrical plugs are the three prong diagonal type plugs as used in New Zealand. Incidentally, the power supply in general is less reliable than the states, and if you bring along your laptop, be sure and bring a surge protector. If you are venturing beyond Rarotonga, the power supply fluctuates to the point that even a surge protector might not protect your laptop. Even the slightest chance of a computer crash makes all writers break out in a sweat, I purchased a variety of converters and plug adaptors and it took me two days to become confident enough to plug my laptops nine volt converter into the local current. Turns out my laptop runs on 110 or 220 and I didn't need the converter, but I did purchase a 220-surge protector from **Pacific Computers Ph. 20-727.** The owner, Grant Walker is an ex-patriot and he was quite helpful solving my power problems and fears.

If you are visiting one of the outer islands don't be surprised if the fan goes off at noon or the lights go out at midnight, Manihiki, Rakahanga and Penrhyn have electric service from 6 to 12, morning and evening, so half of the day is without electricity

Driver's License

The Cook Islands do not recognize any other country when it comes to driver's licenses. They do a booming business in the sale of driver's licenses. I think it offsets trade imbalances and provides employment for an islander or two. The unofficial explanation of this need for a local license is that since New Zealand won't recognize a Cook Island license, the Cook Islands damn well won't recognize a New Zealand license. This international debate seems to be all in good fun and the bonus is that your picture on the local license is a great souvenir and only costs NZ$10.00.

Go to the police station to obtain your license, it's at the east end of Avarua, just before you reach the traffic circle coming from the west. Once you have paid your money, passed the test and had your picture taken your license will be ready in half an hour. I hope the California Department of Motor vehicles is reading this and takes notice.

If you want to rent a scooter or motorcycle, the culmination of the licensing fun is the road test you will need to take on your rental scooter once you apply for your license. The test consists of riding down to the roundabout turning around and riding back without killing yourself, a dog, or a pedestrian. Upon successful completion of this task your smile is sure to fade when you burn your leg on the exhaust pipe of the scooter dismounting. Never mind you have your souvenir license as well as your souvenir burn.

If you should fail the test, and I must add that I have heard of only one person (yes, you Jeff) that has failed, you must push your motorbike back where you rented it, and you will become the topic of discussion at happy hour island-wide. Perhaps if you fail the driving test, you may want to consider **Aitutaki** for the balance of your stay in the Cook Islands, besides the scooter license only costs NZ$2.50 over there.

Telephone

As is the case in most of the world today, the Cook Islands have a reliable phone service. I think we have chucked enough satellites up to the stratosphere to allow quality phone communication worldwide. That being said there are a few peculiarities of their system. Forget the old 911 for emergencies, for police use 999, for ambulance 998, to report a fire 996. For international calls, dial 00 for the international access code, a country code (United States and Canada 1) (Great Britain 44) an area code (406 Montana) and then the however many digit phone number. Thus, if you wanted to call your uncle in Botswana, you would dial (00)(267) 555-1212. Assuming all the satellites are lined up and you're lucky, you at least have a fairly good chance of getting hold of his voice mail. The Cooks' country code is (682) and local numbers are five digit. If you call the Cooks' avoid overlapping voices, there is a time delay on calls from overseas. You may want to adopt the old CB jargon and announce "over" when you complete your sentence. Breaker, Breaker, come in Rarotonga! If you want to send or receive faxes and your hotel does not have facilitates, you can send and receive faxes at the Telecom Cook Islands Office, off the main road in Avarua. Turn right past the police station and proceed two blocks, it will be on your left just as the road turns to the right. If you want to pay for the calls you make, The Cook Islands have phone cards, which are available at the Telecom Office, Post Office and most hotels and shops. They can be used for both local and international calls and work from both public and private phones. You merely dial in the code 147 and then enter your card number and listen for the instructions. The cards come in a variety of denominations from NZ$5.00 to NZ$50.00, just purchase the card based on your anticipated use and you will never be surprised with a hefty charge on your account back home.

Internet Access

If the phone frustrates you, you can use the modern E-mail method of communication. In Avarua, Internet connections are available at numerous locations, with the advent of Wifi to Rarotonga, the number of cyber cafés have plummeted. There is a small location just before you reach Muri beach near Avarua passage. **Summerfield Systems Ph. 23-885** at the bus stop in Cook's Corner has an air-conditioned cyber café, as does **The Internet Shop Ph. 20-728** in Browns Arcade in uptown Avarua. Telecom Cook Islands has a 24-hour booth available for NZ$1.75 for five minutes. If you plan an extended visit and brought along your laptop,

In the last year, Telecom Cook Islands has added wireless capability to its Internet service in Rarotonga. There are currently seven wifi hot sots on the island. If you start in Avarua there are hot spots at the Telecom office, Telepost, the Port Authority office at the Avitua Harbor as well as the Rarotonga Airport. On the west side of the island the Edgewater Resort, Rarotongan Resort and Aroa's Beachside Inn all have the service. In the Muri Beach area, the Muri Beach Resort and Muri Beach Club Resort are the only locations. While these nine spots offer the service, I am sure in the near future additional spots will be added Nearly all laptops produced in the past three year feature Wifi capability as a standard feature so it is just a matter of time before the Cook Islands embrace the technology. One concept Telecom has failed to embrace is the *free* wireless. In order to access their Wifi you will need to purchase a Prepaid Wifi card, which as you may have guessed is available at the locations given above. These cards come in a variety of denominations, based on those pesky megabites. A basic 50 MB card costs NZ$15.00 and they are also available in 150, 250, and up to 400 MB cards costing NZ$64.00. So it pays to try and determine your usage during your stay before purchasing a card. If you are just checking your E-Mails and not uploading pictures, you can probably get by with a less expensive card, depending on how long you are visiting. The fact that the Wifi cards usage is based on the volume of data transferred, rather than time online, is a bit of a nuisance, but you can view the usage statistics by logging onto a website shown on the card. If you are traveling to Atiu, there is a Wifi network at the bar of Atiu Villas. Talk to the owners about rates, I failed to discuss it during my visit.

Taxes

One of the most annoying customs in the islands, and one that I could personally do without, are taxes. They exist and persist like a zealous mosquito, taking a constant bite out of your wallet. A government mandated value added tax of 12.5% is added to almost everything in the Cook Islands. When comparing prices or determining cost, always ask if the price includes the value added tax or VAT. Know and understand your bill before payment to insure there are few surprises on your final check. Most lodgings include all taxes in the rates they quote, so at least the bite of the taxman is hidden from the consumer.

Tipping

Keep in mind that tipping is not the custom in the Cook Islands and should only be added if the service was superior. Do you remember the movie, *"Pay it forward"?* Well the Cook Islanders embraced this theory long before the movie. It is part of their nature to help others and they feel it will be returned in the end and I think that is why tipping has never caught on in this region. So pay it forward traveler!

The prices shown or quoted are the price that is to be paid, unlike some parts of the world, haggling over prices is considered rude in the Cook Islands.

Food

In general the food in the Cook's is quite good, though as in most remote island locations, is somewhat limited. Most food arrives via New Zealand, so look for a lot of lamb at the meat counter. Locally produced items like seafood and fruits are readily available and are very reasonably priced. Food prices in general are higher than Stateside, but since most accommodations provide cooking facilities, it is still more economical to prepare your own meals. Look in the restaurant section of this book for places to eat. The **CITC Food Center** near the harbor and **Foodland Supermarket** on the main road near the ANZ bank are the choices in Avarua, with CITC getting the edge on prices. On the South side of the island it's **Wigmore's Super Store**. The name may be a bit overstated, but they have a wide selection of goods if your lodging is on the southern part of Rarotonga. The **Cook Island Liquor Supplies** near the airport has the best selection and lowest prices for adult beverages. There are an amazingly wide variety of wines from all over the world; import duties make New Zealand wines the least expensive choices. There are many small convenience stores surrounding the island for picking up what you forgot at the market. The prices are only slightly higher and the convenience is well worth it. Don't be surprised if the mini-marts have better pricing on locally grown fruits and vegetables, almost all islanders have a substantial home garden and sell the excess to their neighbor, the convenience store operator.

Water

The water in the Cook Islands tastes great and is probably superior to anything we drink at home. The water is untreated and if you are sensitive to water purification you may want to boil your drinking water. On the outer islands it is best to ask before drinking water from the tap. Bottled *Vaima* water is available in most locations, *Vaima* is Cook Islands Maori for "pure water," the bottled water is basically rainwater that flows down from the hills and is captured in catchments in the valley, where it is allowed to settle and is then UV filtered and bottled. This bottled water is available at most stores throughout the island in a variety of sizes. Return your empty bottle to the factory and they will refill it for a nominal charge. As they say, refill, recycle, and reduce waste. Imagine attempting this process stateside, local health officials would have a field day, lawyers would question the purity of the water, the paperwork from the lawsuits would create far more waste than the water savings. Sometimes it is easier to accomplish things on a small island, where the consumer takes on some of the responsibility.

Health

There are no specific health problems in the islands. The mosquitoes on occasion carry dengue fever, which is probably the most serious health concern present in the Cook Islands. Take a good insect repellant with you to the islands, as the cost of the repellant is generally cheaper than purchasing it locally. Most lodging is subject to shore breezes that keep the mosquitoes at bay. They are more of a problem the further inland you travel.

Use common sense with your health in the tropics; over exertion can cause heat stroke and dehydration. Sunburn can be a real problem, especially if you are light skinned and prone to burn. It is best to ease into sun exposure over your stay, avoid prolonged exposure and wear a shirt and hat for the majority of the time spent at the beach or on sunny patios. Bring a good sunscreen (SP15) and wear sunglasses. If you do burn, try the local Mauke Miracle Oil for pain relief, preferably with a New Zealand Steinlager beer on the side.

As a result of my legendary freighter trip to the northern islands, I returned suffering from extreme dehydration and fatigue, low blood sugar and low blood pressure and after fainting twice made a trip to the government health clinic just outside Avarua, where I was seen by a local physician who took my blood pressure and sampled my blood and as a result told me to stop taking my blood pressure pills, resume taking my diabetes medications and gave me a prescription for an antibiotic for the nasty infection in my leg. That visit, the prescription and a follow up visit two days later cost me a total of NZ$62.00. They only laughed when I tried to use my Blue Cross card, I can hardly wait to get back and file for reimbursement.

What Time Is It? What Day Is It?

The Cook Islands are in the same time zone as Hawaii, which means they are two hours earlier than the West Coast of the United States, but if the US is on daylight savings time, they are three hours early. New Zealand time is two hours earlier, but in New Zealand it is the next day, as they are east of the International Date Line. I wouldn't worry about time, as island travelers know, the pace of life dictates "Island Time" or "Maori Time" as it is called in the Cook's. To further confuse you, the date June 15, 2003 is shown as 15/6/03, instead of the US version of 6/15/03. Don't worry; be happy, you will figure it out when you get there. Just keep in mind that your return flight does not depart on "Maori Time". As an example of 'Maori time', the New Years fireworks occurred on the night of January 18th. The fireworks were repeatedly postponed for various reasons including cyclones and rain. Rest assured that the fireworks, if not timely, were a glorious display, lighting the sky over the lagoon in Avarua and welcoming the New Year in "island time."

Mail Service

You best send your postcards the first day you arrive as it takes about ten days to two weeks for mail to be delivered to the United States. The post office is on Takuvaine Road in Avarua, but you can leave outgoing mail with the front desk where you are staying. If you expect to receive mail, the Post Office will facilitate General Delivery, but the US Postal Service, lacking in geographic knowledge, has a history of sending things to the Cocos Islands or Costa Rica. Underline Cook Islands and South Pacific to improve chances of a timely delivery. Postal rates to North America are NZ$.90 for a postcard and NZ$1.15 for a letter up to 5 grams.

Courtesies and Appropriate Dress

I think most view the South Pacific as an informal, laid back environment. While this is true to some extent, there are rules of dress and behavior that should be adhered to while visiting the islands. The wearing of swimsuits should be limited to pool or beach areas. You will notice that native islanders wear long pants and formal shirts in town or on the bus; you should dress so as to respect this custom. I would be the last to suggest that you take along long pants, but you should have a pair if you plan on attending church services, which is a highly recommended activity. For the bus or in town, shorts and a shirt should be worn at all times away from the beach. Women should wear a cover up over bathing suits if in town or traveling on the bus. Men should wear clothing to respect the islanders, it does not mean you need to wear pants or formal shirts, but shorts should be Bermuda type and not cut-offs and men's shirts should have sleeves.

When you wander into a shop or a market, always greet the storekeeper with a 'good morning' or other introduction. It is considered rude to walk into a shop and just ask for what you desire without first offering some sort of acknowledgement. It's a small thing and something that we should probably do anyway, but it is especially important in the islands. This small formality will show that you respect them as a person and not just a salesperson.

Crime

No place is without it, but I must say that in the two months I lived in the Cook Islands I saw little evidence of crime and read few accounts of crime in the local papers. I think the visitor should take due care to protect his valuables, for if wallets and cameras are left unattended, it is only an invitation for theft. Most of the hotels have a safe for your traveler's checks and cash. I suggest you leave behind the fancy jewelry with the fancy clothes, women may want to bring along a minimum of accessories and there is little need for formal wear in the islands. I was concerned about my rental motorbike, but the clerk assured me that, as long as I didn't leave the key in it, it would be fine.

Taking Pictures

Ask first when taking a Cook Islanders photo, this is just basic courtesy and most islanders are happy to oblige. Film, though more expensive, is readily available in Rarotonga. However on the out islands you may not be able to buy film and film is generally sent back to Rarotonga for processing. Film processing in Rarotonga is available at both **Fuji Image Centre Ph. 26-238**, they are just past Cook's Corner and before you get to the telecom office, or **CITC Photo Ph. 22-000,** in the CITC Shopping Center on the main road next to the ANZ bank. Both places above have complete services, including one-hour and digital services, prints, enlargements and copying digital photos to a CD.

Sunday

Cook islanders have considered Sunday to be a day of rest ever since the coming of the missionaries in the mid-eighteenth century. Most commercial services are closed on Sunday. Banks, businesses, bus service and most restaurants are closed. Air travel between the islands comes to a halt and even the golf course shuts down for the day. Most islanders attend one of the many branches of the **Cook Islands Christian Church** or CICC as it is commonly referred to locally. Church services begin at 10:00 and last until 11:30 and the hymnal singing in the Christian churches of the Cook Islands is known throughout the South Pacific. Locations are island wide and there is usually a CICC church located within walking distance of wherever you are staying on the island. Local women wear their finest and top it off with their handmade *Rito* hats from the outer islands. The pageant of church service is quite moving and a must see for the visitor.

In addition to the Christian Church, the Catholic and Mormon religions have churches and a strong following in the Cook Islands and, to a lesser degree, the Seventh Day Adventist Church.

Newspapers and Magazines

The *Cook Island News* **www.cinews.co.ck** is published daily except Sunday and although quite brief, provides a wealth of information on events and happenings island wide. If your trip is in the planning stage visit their website to get up to date on the local issues. When you do arrive in the islands and buy the paper, you will find a brief recap of the World's news as well as the listing of International plane arrivals and departures, shipping arrival and departures and even a spot that indicates if the old Dow Jones is up or down back in the states. There is a classified section and even a daily crossword, to pass your time in the islands. Much space in the paper is dedicated to local politics and I find this section extremely interesting, proving that politics is the same worldwide. Whoever is in office is wrong and whoever is challenging has the answer. That is until the next election when the roles are reversed. There is a "Sunday" paper on Rarotonga, the *Cook Island Herald*, though published on Saturday; it is weekly so I am calling this the Sunday paper. If you insist on a major newspaper, the **New Zealand Herald** is available at Bounty Bookstore the day after publication, arriving on the daily Air New Zealand flight from Auckland. In addition to the two above there is the **Cook Island Sun**, which is published periodically and is basically a tourist publication with no news value. What the Sun does offer, is a lot of information and specials for tours and restaurants of interest to the visitor; you can pick up the Sun on arrival at the airport or island wide in hotels restaurants or the tourism office.

T.V. & Radio

Well there is television and radio on Rarotonga, but don't get it in your mind you will have a selection of stations on either. The television consists of one station and broadcasting begins at various times depending on the day. Monday through Friday between Noon and 2:00 PM is Christian Programming, followed by the Australia Network Programming rebroadcast in the afternoon until about 6:00 PM. Local programming returns at 7:00 PM with local news, sports and weather. At 8:00 PM weekdays locals are perched in front of the TV for the New Zealand soap opera "Shortland Street" a long running epic which is fun to watch if you can put up with the pathetically inept local TV ads which pepper the commercial breaks. Late at night you can pick up the odd rugby match from New Zealand. The weekly Cook Islands Herald has the all the listings; you can pick it up at various locations on the island.

Radio has three channels, **Radio Cook Islands www.radio.co.ck** broadcasts at 630khz AM or FM 89.9 and can be heard on most southern group islands, while **Matriki FM** broadcasts at 91.9, 96.7 and 99.9 mhz FM and has a range limited to parts of Rarotonga. **Ocean & Earth FM** broadcasts at 101.1 mhz FM. Music programming on FM, is quite interesting, Eminem may be followed by, Ray Charles who may precede, Willie Nelson, so don't be put off by one song and think the foremast is country western, they play it all mixed in with the Vaimutu Stars and other regional groups. It's worth noting that Matriki FM lists "no rap" in their advertising, a trend that Papa Mike certainly supports. The Cook Islands Herald lists the AM program, which appears to be a bit more serious and offers traditional AM fare, talk shows, weather, news and a top twenty show.

Most locals opt for watching videos, which can be rented at various locations on Rarotonga. Some of the upscale accommodations have videos in the room or have a lounge with a TV and a VCR for guest use. If all else fails the rental locations are happy to rent you a TV and VCR

Maps

You will find few and very general maps in this guidebook, the "print on demand format" of this book and my abilities limit the maps within the book. Full color detailed maps of Rarotonga, Aitutaki, Atiu and Mangaia are available free of charge from the tourist office in Avarua, or by mail on request. Maps are also available in the periodical tourist publication the *Cook Islands Sun*, which is available island wide on Rarotonga.

Planning Your Trip

Ask ten people where the Cook Islands are located and you will receive ten different answers, none of which is likely to be the correct answer. So before we plan your trip we should have a little geography lesson as to where the Cook Islands are located. For the record, the Cook Islands are located between Tahiti and Samoa, 3000 miles directly south of the Hawaiian Islands. So take a look at the map below, so that you will have an idea where you are going before we plan your trip

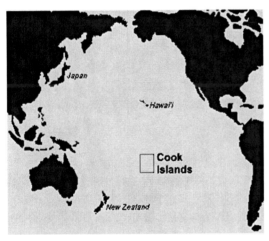

While all the planning in the world will not guarantee the perfect vacation, knowledge of your destination will definitely help you avoid many potential pitfalls. With his said, you have already taken a giant step toward preparation; after all, you did purchase this guidebook. Your largest expense will be your airfare and listed below are options from various start points around the world. An extra hour or two spent searching out bargains in airfare can save you more than any other item in your budget, so ask around, read the paper, search the internet and find a travel agent who is well versed on Rarotonga and the Cook Islands.

United States

As you are probably aware, airfares fluctuate about as much as the U.S. Stock Market, with fare revisions on a daily basis. For your trip to the Cook Islands, I have some good news and some bad news. The good news is you currently have only a single airline to deal with, **Air New Zealand Ph. (800) 262-1234 www.airnz.com** The bad news is you have only one airline to deal with, which in some ways, limits competition. If you are traveling from the United States your only option is to fly the twice-weekly Air New Zealand non-stop to Rarotonga. All Air New Zealand flights depart Los Angeles mid-evening and arrive very early the next morning. If you have the time you may want to look into including a trip to New Zealand on your visit to the Cook Islands, as the additional airfare is minimal. Another approach is to catch the **Air Rarotonga Ph. (682) 22-888 www.airraro.com** twice-weekly flight aboard their 70-seat ATR-72 turboprop from Papeete in Tahiti to Rarotonga, which is currently scheduled for Tuesdays and Saturdays. Service to Tahiti is offered by a variety of airlines from the United States and South America. If you live near a major U.S. city, check the travel section of the Sunday paper; on occasion they advertise special package prices on trips to Rarotonga and Aitutaki.

Canada

If you are traveling from Canada, **Air New Zealand Ph. (800) 663-5494 www.airnewzealand.ca** offers service from Vancouver and Toronto. Canadians are raving about the new non-stop service from Vancouver to Auckland, which allows them to avoid American anti-terrorist security, which is internationally known for it's heavy handed tactics.

Australia/New Zealand

If you are traveling from Australia you will fly **Air New Zealand (Australia) Ph. (1300) 365-525 www.airnz.com.au** (New Zealand) **(09) 377-7999 www.airnewzealand.co.nz** or **Pacific Blue** (Australia) **(Ph. 13-1645)** (New Zealand) **(Ph. 0800-67-0000) www.pacificblue.com** and connect out of Auckland. There are several flights a week to Rarotonga. From New

Zealand you will fly direct from Auckland. Australians loathe connecting through Auckland and there is talk about creating direct flights from Australia, but at the time of writing there is no direct connection to the Cook Islands from Australia. You will find that buying package tours may be your best bet from Australia and New Zealand, try **Hideaway Holidays Ph. 02-9743-0253 www.hidewayholidays.com.au** for packages or search the Internet for the best deals.

UK/Europe

Travel from the United Kingdom and Europe is quite an undertaking when you consider that you can't get much further away from the Cook Islands than these locations. That is why I am amazed that, according to tourist board information, three times as many people from the U.K. and Europe travel to Rarotonga as visit from the United States. I guess most of us Yanks just don't get past Hawaii. Travel from London on Air New Zealand; they have direct flights to Los Angeles that connect with the flights to Rarotonga. From continental Europe, Air New Zealand has direct flights from Frankfurt to Los Angeles, which connect to the Cook Islands. You may want to look into around the world or circle pacific fares if you have come this far and you have the time, you may as well see a lot more of the planet.

South America

From South America you can catch the **LAN Chile Airlines Ph. (600) 526-2000 www.lanchile.com** flight from Santiago, Chile to Papeete, Tahiti and from there catch the twice-weekly Air Rarotonga flight to Rarotonga. The Lan Chile flight currently stops in Easter Island on it's way to Tahiti, which I think would be a fun stopover on your way to the Cook's.

Other Resources

When pricing tickets, be sure to ask if fares change close to the times you are traveling. Sometimes moving departure or return by a day or two will substantially reduce the cost of a ticket. The ticket prices listed above were current at the time I wrote this and were updated right up until the book went to the printer, but use them only as a guide, for I am sure most will be obsolete by the time you purchase this book.

Once you research fares on the two airlines above, you may wish to contact a travel agent and inquire about package deals. There are a host of consolidators that offer packages combining airfare with accommodations, that in some cases is less than what you would pay for airfare alone. Some of the major consolidators are **Sunspots Ph. (800) 334-5623** or visit their website at **www.sunspotsintl.com** or try **Discover Wholesale Travel Ph. (866) 215-4627**, on the web at **www.discovertravel.com** a third based out of Australia is **Hideaway Holidays Ph. (61) 2-9743-0253**, there website is **www.hideawayholidays.com.au/** Your local travel agent will likely have or be able to obtain brochures on a variety of different accommodations, including many that are listed in this guidebook. You may also want to check packages at **Costco**; the huge retailer has packages to Rarotonga and Aitutaki, using several different hotels. You can visit them at their Website **www.costcotravel.com** just click on Cook Islands and you can view current packages to the Cook Islands.

At the time this book is written, the harbor in Rarotonga is being dredged and there is talk of small cruise ships visiting the island. For now the only reasonable way of reaching the islands is by air, that is unless you have a yacht, I seem to have misplaced mine!

Travel to the Outer Islands

If you have the time, resources and/or inclination, my hope is that you will, travel to any of the small outer islands in the Cook chain. The islands are spread out over a rather large geographic area and travel is by small plane or inter-island shipping. For the adventurous, a trip to the outer islands can be a great addition to your experience in paradise. The accommodations at all but Aitutaki are basic but clean, but the hospitality and friendliness of the people offsets any lack of comforts. Refer to each individual island's section in the book. It is possible to arrange visits to combinations of islands, including accommodations, by booking a package. Contact Island Hopper Vacations Ph. 22-026 **www.islandhoppervacations.com** Jetsave Travel Ph. 27-707, **www.jetsave.co.ck** or Timpani Tours Ph. 25-266, Website **www.tipanitours.com** for detailed information on travel to the outer islands see the Inter Island Travel section of this guidebook. The popularity of the Internet, in some cases may allow you to book directly with the lodging of your choice. Look for websites and E-Mail addresses in the Where To Stay section of each individual island. Keep in mind that E-Mail responses will take up to a week, as the Internet access is likely through the school or government office on the island, outside of Rarotonga, Aitutaki and Atiu, there is no wireless reception, so be patient when attempting booking.

Air travel is via **Air Rarotonga Ph. 22-888**; there are four flights daily to **Aitutaki**, a single daily flight direct to **Mitiaro**, **Atiu**, and **Mauke** (after a stop on Mitiaro). Service to **Mangaia** is four times a week on Monday, Wednesday, Friday and Saturday. The islands in the northern group are served far less frequently, with one weekly flight to **Manihiki** on Thursday and one weekly flight to **Penrhyn** on Saturday. Air Rarotonga has no scheduled flights on Sunday. The islands in the southern group are only an hour away by plane, with the two northern group islands 3-4 hours by plane. It is now possible to travel between Atiu and Aitutaki, without having to return to Rarotonga, flights are limited, currently available on Wednesdays only. With limited seats on this flight, it is recommended that you book this flight at least a month in advance. For that matter if you plan on taking inter-island flights I suggest you make them over the Internet prior to leaving for your vacation. The Air Raro website is very easy to use, with prices listed for all flights. A visit to the smaller islands in the Southern Group is a real treat, where you may very well be the only tourist on the island for your stay, so book ahead to avoid sold out flights on these small panes. Note that the frequency of inter island flights above represents peak months, flight frequency is reduce during slow periods. Refer to additional warnings at the bottom of the section on inter-island flights for additional information. Air Rarotonga has occasional special fares to the outer islands; you can sign up for their E-Mail alerts by sending a blank E-Mail to, **specialfares-on@airraro.co.ck.** The fares are available on last minute travel only, so you will need to be in Rarotonga or arriving within a few days to take advantage of these fares.

What You Will Need To Take On Your Trip

Clothes

Half of what you think you need is a good rule of thumb. Dress in the Cook Islands is casual and everyone wears t-shirts and shorts in the daytime. At night men may want to wear cotton knit golf shirts or tropical patterned "Hawaiian", type shirts. In the evening, women tend to wear sundresses or an island *pareu,* as a skirt or sarong. Sneakers, with or without socks for the men and sandals for the ladies seem to be in vogue. Bring reef walkers for trudging in the lagoon or over the rough native *makatea* coral, and you may want to bring a light jacket or sweater for the evenings. Obviously, you need your swimsuit and a hat for the mid-day sun. If you plan on attending a local church, it is customary for men to wear long pants and women to wear a conservative dress, please respect the island custom.

As I mentioned in the first paragraph, bring half of what you think you need. Four to six t-shirts, 2-4 collared shirts and 4-6 pair of shorts was all I brought for a two-month stay. T-shirts can be bought on Rarotonga, all the way to 5XL and the island is one of the few that I've seen in my travels; which actually have tasteful designs. T-shirts make great souvenirs and the bonus is you only need to transport them one way.

Snorkels, Mask & Fins

What a pain these contraptions are. They take up loads of space in our bag and make our clothes smell like Jacque Cousteau's locker. Many of the guesthouses and hotels in the Cook Islands furnish these to their guests, so check with where you are staying, in hopes you can leave these things home with the dog. In addition you can rent these items on Rarotonga and Aitutaki. If you are similar in size to Shaquille O'Neil and wear a size 16 (American) shoe, you may want to bring your own fins anyway.

I wear glasses and it's always a toss up for me, to take off my glasses so that I can allegedly "see" underwater with my mask. So most of the time I snorkel with my glasses on in order to recognize "Jaws" from a nine-year-old child. Frankly, I never liked putting something on my face that I just spit into; so don't look for me on the Calypso.

Stuff

Comedian George Carlin does a great skit on modern man and his, "stuff", so I will use this area to describe some of the other things you may want to bring along on this South Pacific odyssey. Sunglasses are important not only for noon on the beach, but they allow you to discretely people watch during happy hour. Remember guys the girls with the flowers behind their right ear are the single girls.

Suntan lotion, prescription drugs and insect repellant are welcome additions to your stuff. You will likely want to bring a camera to record the odyssey. Bring a few books for the time on the beach and reading on the plane. Bring along a carry on bag for your trips to the beach and for transporting items on your motorbike, for the rental motorbike fleet on Rarotonga does not come equipped with the basket option. While nobody wants to bring a glass on vacation, you may want to bring along an insulated plastic glass to avoid a puddle on the table when you have a drink with ice, don't laugh, it's a humidity thing. You may also wish to bring along some "anti itch" medication, just in case you forgot to bring along the insect repellant on one of your outings.

Children

This is strictly an option and don't feel that you have to go out and adopt if you don't presently have children. Children will love Rarotonga and the Cook islands. They will swim, paddle and play as children do the world over. Lets face it, we're jealous and it's a great gig for them. The many lagoons are safe and calm and they can snorkel to their hearts content. Be sure and tell them not to touch or break the coral as they play, not only is it protected, but also some varieties can cause serious infections. If or when you attend an island night celebration, your kids are in for a real treat, the performers will interact with them and they will be captivated by the music and costumes.

Tiny babies may not be so fun. Perhaps they are a permanent reminder of your *last* vacation. Rarotonga is packed with baby food and disposable diapers for those little bundles of joy. As a note, Air New Zealand has a couple of bassinets on each of their 767-300 flights. You will need to notify them in advance, but there is no additional cost for this. Just keep in mind the service is on a first come first served basis. Many accommodations offer babysitting, so mom and dad can have a night away from baby.

Now, on to those young adults, the modern teenager and how best to deal with them in paradise, a place they will likely dismiss due to lack of fast food options. I think it's best to let them have their music, but earphones only, please! Without their music they will likely have driven you crazy before you exit the plane. Additionally, I wouldn't mention the lack of television on Rarotonga until they have sealed the door of the plane and you have safely left the terminal. Seriously, this may or may not be the situation, but if they are a pain, it will not be for lack of things to do. They can dive, fish, safari, and swim to name just a few. In most cases, tour operators pick up the guests at their hotel and return them at the end of the day, allowing them to enjoy their trip as well as allowing you to enjoy your time.

Food Items

While there is an ample and varied food selection in the Cook Islands, there are several items you may want to bring along. Air New Zealand currently has a baggage allowance of 100 lbs per person in two bags and no matter how many t-shirts and shorts I pack I have plenty of weight left, so I bring along a sealed cooler in which I freeze a bag of sirloin steaks and several pounds of bacon. Mark the cooler with your name and destination lodging and then seal it all up with duct and clear plastic tape. You are permitted to bring these items into the Cook Islands and beef is in short supply on Rarotonga and extremely scarce on the outer islands. The bacon is permitted, but pork is not permitted, the bacon is cured and therefore, somehow allowed into the islands. The Kiwi peanut butter is a bit bland to my taste so I bring along the biggest jar of Skippy extra chunky in my bag as well as a bottle of Heinz Catsup, to replace the New Zealand Waddies brand, which is, shall we say, an acquired taste and not for Papa Mike. The final item is a generous supply of your favorite coffee. The locally grown Atiu coffee is OK but a bit expensive and not to my taste. Locals consider Nescafe to be just as good as real coffee; so don't look for Starbucks anytime soon.

What Not To Take

Leave behind your hash pipe, fruits, cats, dogs and your nine-millimeter Uzi, for none of these are permitted.

Finally and seriously, let's make sure we leave behind our Western expectations on the flight down, try and relax and come to grips with the slower pace of life that will happen when the door of the plane opens. Especially Americans, I am generalizing, but as a group, we have a way of *demanding* service rather than simple requesting it. Smile at that shopkeeper, ask him how he or she is doing or comment about the weather, to do otherwise is considered rude in their culture. Keep in mind that patience is indeed a virtue.

Inter Island Transportation

Air

For most visitors considering inter-island travel **Air Rarotonga Ph. 22-888 Fax. 23-288 www.airraro.com** is the first and pretty much only option. There are four flights daily to Aitutaki, but service to other islands is much less frequent and not all islands have daily service. There are two weekly flights to the northern group, one each to Manihiki on Thursday and one weekly to Penrhyn on Saturday. Air Rarotonga flies 18-passenger twin turbo prop Bandierante planes which

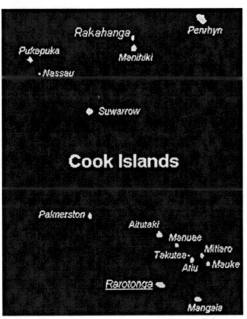

are relatively quiet and reliable. Flights to the southern group take roughly one hour, while flights to Manihiki and Penrhyn are a rather cramped 3-1/2 to 4 hours in length. All Rarotonga travel agents offer package tours to the southern group of islands, which combine airfare and accommodations. Rates vary substantially and tickets bought in the islands are substantially less than those bought prior to arrival. The problem is that if you wait to buy your inter island tickets after you arrive, you risk the chance of the flights being sold out. I wouldn't worry too much if you are only going to Aitutaki, as there are four daily flights, but if you plan on purchasing one of Air Rarotonga's multi-island passes, you may have a problem. You make the call, if you have a lot of flexibility you can wait till you arrive, if not book ahead. Go to Air Rarotonga's Website listed above for up to date pricing and descriptions of their Discovery Pass and Pacific Island Pass packages. Route information is listed below. For additional information on travel to the outer islands visit the **Travel To The Outer Island** subheading in the **Planning Your Trip** section of this book.

Beware! Having a confirmed reservation does not guarantee that the flight will not be cancelled. Depending on demand, certain flights may suffer cancellation, if bookings do not materialize to make the flight cost effective. This occurred in my Atiu to Aitutaki connecter flight, when the flight was cancelled a couple weeks prior to the flight. Instead I was re-routed on a flight back to Rarotonga and then later that day flown to Aitutaki at no additional cost. The only result was half a day spent in the terminal in Rarotonga, which was not a major problem to me because I had plenty of time in the islands. If you are on a tight schedule, and cannot adjust, it could be a much larger problem. Keep this in mind on flights other than Aitutaki, which has four flights per day and seldom suffers cancellation. The list below mirrors Air Rarotonga's website, but having just returned from the islands, I can tell you that the schedule shown is not currently in effect. The schedule represents the busy part of the year, during slow periods, January to April; you will find fewer flights, than what is shown on their schedule. Air Rarotonga is quite good at notifying you of schedule changes, but the changes may affect your travel plans in a negative manner.

Air Rarotonga
Flights To The Outer Islands

Rarotonga-Aitutaki

Days	Flight #	Departs	Time	Arrives	Time
Mon-Sat	GZ-612	RAR	8:00	AIT	8:50
	GZ-613	AIT	9:10	RAR	10:00
	GZ-614	RAR	10:30	AIT	11:20
	GZ-615	AIT	11:40	RAR	12:30
	GZ-616	RAR	2:00	AIT	2:50
	GZ-617	AIT	3:05	RAR	3:50
	GZ-618	RAR	4:30	AIT	5:20
	GZ-619	AIT	5:40	RAR	6:30

Rarotonga-Other Islands

Days	Flight #	Departs	Time	Arrives	Time
Monday	GZ-696	RAR	10:30	MOI	11:20
	GZ-696	MOI	11:40	MUK	11:50
	GZ-696	MUK	12:10	RAR	1:00
	GZ-636	RAR	1:00	AIU	1:45
	GZ-637	AIU	2:05	RAR	2:50
	GZ-676	RAR	1:30	MGS	2:10
	GZ-677	MGS	2:30	RAR	3:10

Days	Flight #	Departs	Time	Arrives	Time
Tuesday	GZ-634	RAR	10:30	AIU	11:15
	GZ-626	AIU	11:35	AIT	12:25
	GZ-625	AIT	12:45	AIU	1:35
	GZ-635	AIU	1:35	RAR	2:40
	GZ-656	RAR	1:00	MUK	1:50
	GZ-657	MUK	2:10	RAR	3:00

Days	Flight #	Departs	Time	Arrives	Time
Wednesday	GZ-676	RAR	1:30	MGS	2:10
	GZ-677	MGS	2:30	RAR	3:10
	GZ-656	RAR	1:00	MUK	1:50
	GZ-657	MUK	2:10	RAR	3:00
	GZ-697	RAR	10:30	AIU	11:15
	GZ-697	AIU	11:35	MOI	11:45
	GZ-697	MOI	12:05	RAR	12:55

Days	Flight #	Departs	Time	Arrives	Time
Thursday	GZ-696	RAR	10:30	MOI	11:20

Days	Flight #	Departs	Time	Arrives	Time
	GZ-696	MOI	11:40	MUK	11:50
	GZ-696	MUK	12:10	RAR	3:00
	GZ-636	RAR	1:00	AIU	1:45
	GZ-637	AIU	2:05	RAR	2:50
	GZ-710	RAR	6:00	MHX	9:40
	GZ-711	MHX	10:40	RAR	2:20

Days	Flight #	Departs	Time	Arrives	Time
Friday	GZ-636	RAR	1:00	AIU	1:45
	GZ-637	AIU	2:05	RAR	2:50
	GZ-676	RAR	1:30	MGS	2:10
	GZ-677	MGS	2:30	RAR	3:10
	GZ-654	RAR	10:30	MUK	11:20
	GZ-655	MUK	11:40	RAR	12:30

Days	Flight #	Departs	Time	Arrives	Time
Saturday	GZ-676	RAR	1:30	MGS	2:10
	GZ-677	MGS	2:30	RAR	3:10
	GZ-700	RAR	6:00	PYE	10:00
	GZ-701	PYE	11:00	RAR	3:00
	GZ-634	RAR	10:30	AIU	11:15
	GZ-635	AIU	11:35	RAR	12:20

Island Codes

RAR	Rarotonga	MUK	Mauke	
AIT	Aitutaki	MHX	Manihiki	
AIU	Atiu	MGS	Mangaia	
MOI	Mitiaro	PYE	Penrhyn	

Note: There are no flights on Sunday

Sea

There is this romantic notion about traveling the South Seas in a tramp steamer, drifting from port to port a true vagabond in paradise. I think for the most part it is a myth, but it is still possible to travel inter-island in the Cook Islands by freighter. Elliot Smith in his book, *Cook Islands Companion*, described freighter travel to the out islands thusly, "I slept with a t-shirt over my face to absorb the fumes and smells and ate only bread and jam to avoid stomach problems". Of course that was ten years ago and I'm hopeful passenger comfort has improved. He went on to mention that, "There's nothing quite like gazing at the Southern Cross followed by waking to a tropical island on the horizon". I suspect the good outweighs the lack of comfort and there is always a price to pay for adventure.

So if you are indeed adventurous and have the time, steamer passage to the outer islands can be the adventure of a lifetime. On the other hand, it could become two weeks in hell. You must keep in mind that the purpose of a freighter is to deliver freight to the outer islands. Thus freight is their top priority, it determines when they leave, where they go and how long they stay. If cyclone Shaquille O'Neil decides to make an appearance during your trip, you may end up off Pukapuka, riding out the storm for a week. With this in mind and time on your hands, here is how you go about preparing for your great adventure.

Go by **Taio Shipping Ltd Ph. (682) 24-905 Fax. (682) 24-906**, they have an E-mail address of **Taio@oyster.net.ck** their offices are located at Avatiu harbor, behind the Port Authority building on the right. Talk to the clerk and find out the shipping schedule. She will be able to tell you when they are closing freight for the next trip. Once they stop accepting freight, she will then know what islands they are going to and when the freighter will depart. Departure time and date will probably change at least twice, so you will drive your hotel nuts, trying to figure out exactly when you will be leaving. You need to be flexible, because the boat won't leave until the perishables are aboard and that is a complex process between Taio and CITC Grocery, the likes of which you don't want to know.

Your choice at that point is to book, what I will laughingly refer to as a "cruise", round trip passage on the freighter to all the islands on their schedule and return to Rarotonga.

Your second option is to go ashore on one of the scheduled islands and await the next freighter, which will arrive when enough freight accumulates in Rarotonga to necessitate a stop on your island. If this sounds a little "iffy", it is, but you said you wanted adventure. Keep in mind that the islands of the northern group are scarcely populated and offer little or no services. Check in with the Tourist Authority office if you are planning on traveling to Rakahanga or Nassau, as they may be able to line up a "home stay" for you on these islands. The islands of Pukapuka, Manihiki and Penrhyn have no specific accommodations; refer to each island's section in this book for contacts that can help you obtain accommodations. If you are planning on staying on Suwarrow, good luck and make sure your family knows where you put your will.

There are two types of fares on the freighters; you can ride on deck, sleeping amongst the cargo. This is the passage favored by most islanders, though I think it is favored for it's reduced price rather than any other reason. People that choose this travel, bring along their own food, rather than paying for meals as part of their fare. The cabin fare includes your bunk and meals and is what I chose on my great adventure, but more of that later, for that's an entirely different book, yet to be written.

I would warn the potential ship passenger that conditions on the boat are far less than what we Americans are accustomed to. The *Manu Nui* is no Carnival love boat. The compartments are cramped and feature a fair share of cockroaches. As mentioned above, there is little ventilation and the toilet facilities are cramped, hot and less than clean. Fresh water showers are available, assuming you can shower on a rocking ship. If you are over 6'2" tall, get used to scabs on the top of your head, as light fixtures and doorjambs are built for rugged, tough Scandinavian crews of 5'10" or less. There is one less light fixture at the top of the stairs, after repeatedly being hit, I managed to knock it completely off the ceiling. My recollections are biased, since my trip included a couple rounds with Hurricane Dovi, but just keep in mind that the purpose of the trip is freight and not passengers. While not every trip involves a hurricane, there is considerable wave movement and I recommend the trip to travelers in good general health, agile on their feet and somewhat immune to motion sickness. At the end of this section are lists of items I suggest you take along for the voyage. My last helpful hint, hurricane season is November thru April, mate!

In contrast to the negatives in the last paragraph, I would like to point out that the nearly simultaneous moonset and sunrise on the open seas, on our return voyage from Penrhyn to Rarotonga, was a once in a lifetime experience that I will cherish forever. The memory of the sunrise passage on the outgoing tide into Penhryn's lagoon still brings tears to my eyes, and as we say in America, "everything that doesn't kill you, only makes you stronger." That trip made me a lot stronger.

This brings us to the cost of the great adventure, round trip passage is NZ$795, so for the cost of a weekend in Vegas, you can ply the wild seas. I could create a great chart showing you destinations and costs, but the entire northern group cost the same and I guess there is no real need for a timetable, is there? I must report that the Manu Nui is now at rest on the bottom of the ocean off Rarotonga, as the ship finally succumbed to old age and was laid to rest. At the time this is written Taio Shipping is down to one inter-island freighter as the Maungaroa is perched on the Avaitu Breakwater, the victim of storm winds in January of 2008. Its fate of the Maungaroa is now in question, but the ship was scheduled to be scuttled prior to blowing onto the breakwater. The government is currently negotiating in Norway for a much needed second freighter. Reliable freighter service to the outer islands is a government priority as fuel for airline service, electrical service and needed food supplies all need to reach the outer islands by sea. Hopefully the new freighter will include a few more passenger comforts for those wishing to travel by freighter.

List Of items For Freighter Trip

1. Patience, if you don't bring a major helping of this all else is lost.
2. A good pillow, the one provided is old and well, dead, you understand.
3. Baby powder, for rather obvious reasons.
4. A good large towel, for those rock and roll shower forays.
5. Some clothesline hooks, to dry your laundry.
6. An armful of books, it's a long trip between islands.
7. A bar of soap sounds pretty basic, but I forgot.
8. Dramamine (seasickness pills) super strength if available
9. A good pair of deck shoes for walking on slippery boat decks
10. Bring juice or soft drinks (you can use small fridge in dayroom)
11. You may want to bring a knife and fork (Maori eat with their hands)
12. Napkins or paper towels (don't ask me what the Maori do for this)
13. A portable 220 or battery powered fan might help circulation in the cabin

A Word Or Two About The Food On The Inter Island Freighter

While you can choose to eat with the crew, their nutritional tastes are far different than mine and the cook lacks some imagination in his meal choices.

Breakfast is eggs, usually hardboiled, sometimes fried (don't ask for sunny side up). Usually there is bread and margarine available at the morning meal; we lost our freezer, so ran out of bread for the return trip. There was one great breakfast, the night after the worst of our hurricane nights. Our freezer was tossed about and broken by a huge wave; next morning it was all you can eat raspberry ripple ice cream prior to defrosting; sure beat the hell out of those hard-boiled eggs.

Lunch is Chef's choice soup and his choice never varies, it's salty and I learned to avoid it at all costs. There is also a vegetable, the likes of which most Americans have never viewed. Sometimes *Taro,* a gray potato like bulb, similar in size to a potato. Sometimes the vegetable was *Kuru* or breadfruit, as it is referred to in the rest of the world. My favorite was the purple *Kumara* or Cook Island sweet potato, funny to look at but good tasting.

Dinner was one of three options, the first of which was "chops" which, while sounding good, turned out to be lamb neck chops, a portion of the lamb that surely is not used for human consumption back in the states. Second dinner option was chicken parts. When I say parts, I mean parts, no skinless breasts, mind you, but everything else but the beaks. The chicken was in a sauce that was suspiciously similar to the chef's choice soup, but I had no proof they were the same. Third choice was fish, canned mackerel, for the most part, but supplemented by anything the trolling lines picked up or we caught when anchored off an island. I passed on the mackerel, as I consider this to be bait and not food, but the fish we caught were immediately filleted and fried and tasted great. In addition to the above, we had great hunks of overcooked rice, which at times, looked damn good to me.

Coffee and tea as well as milk were always available. The coffee and milk were evaporated, and though quite popular with the islanders and crew, I admit to being a snob, preferring my coffee to be of the ground variety and my milk to be closer to the

cow than powdered. Besides it was always a life threatening experience to get back and forth from the kitchen to the day room because of the rocking of the ship, never mind that you had to hold the cup the entire time you drank the coffee.
If you are taking the ship for the two-week return trip, take along lots of bottled water or juice. I would suggest a large jar of peanut butter and a couple of jars of jam. Some canned fruit and vegetables would help; don't forget the opener. While alcohol is reputedly not allowed, you can take along a bottle or a couple of six-packs of beer, just keep them in your cabin and don't offer any to the crew. Forget ice cubes, but you can use the day room refrigerator to cool your beer (keep an eye on it, so it doesn't disappear).

Good luck and maybe the chef's choice soup will change by the time you head out on your great adventure.

PART 2
THE ISLANDS

Rarotonga

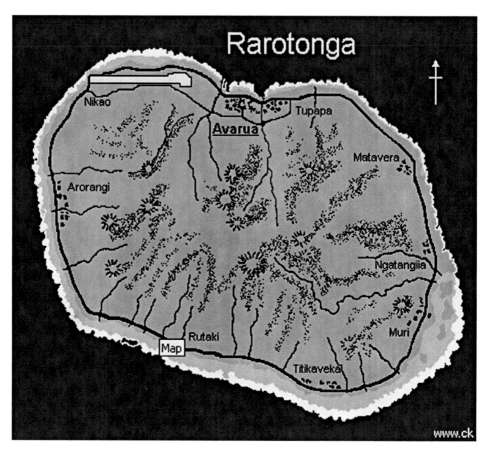

If you fly in to Rarotonga during the day, the beauty of the island unfolds right before you. Your first view is of the barrier reef and the lush green hills that lead to the pointed peeks in the interior of the island. As you get closer, you can make out the palm trees and small homes that dot the shoreline. It becomes immediately apparent that you are arriving in a destination that is quite special and far removed from our western civilization. Your visit to Rarotonga will likely only reinforce that first impression you felt as you arrived.

As you exit the plane you will smell the heat of the tropics, be it 4:30 A.M or middle of the day, the humidity will take you by surprise. As you approach the arrival lounge I can guarantee you will be amazed to hear live music. I know you are sitting out there saying, give me a break, live music at 4:30 A.M.? As far as I know the Rarotongan Don Ho (Jake Numunga) meets all incoming flights, regardless of their arrival time, so yes that music is live. Once you enter the lounge and pass Jake, you will face three immigration lines, keep an eye on the left line labeled returning islanders and fall in behind any locals on your flight, this move will save you a good half hour over anyone that hasn't read this book. After 12 hours on the plane, this tip alone is worth the price of the guidebook.

Immigration and customs take but a few minutes, they review the arrival card you filled out on the plane and ask a few cursory questions based on the information on your card. You are automatically issued a 31-day visitors pass and sent to pick up your bags prior to clearing customs. The customs official will then determine if he wishes to view the contents of your bags or wave you on. In most cases he will welcome you to Rarotonga and send you on your way, you have arrived.

Island Transportation

If you have made previous accommodation reservations, which are technically required for entry into the country, you likely received transfers for your travel to and from the airport. To locate the transfer agent, just proceed to the left out of the terminal, where you will be directed to waiting transportation. If you don't have transfers, I suggest you see the gentlemen from Raro Tours who will either arrange for your transportation or point you towards a taxi. Since the island is only twenty miles in circumference, no hotel is more than ten miles away and cost should be in the NZ$15.00 range. Once you are situated in your hotel, you can decide on options for transportation during your stay.

Taxis

There are plenty of Taxis on Rarotonga, though the government controlled rates at NZ$2.50 per kilometer are rather steep. That's probably why I prefer the bus. A partial list of taxi companies includes 24-hour service from **Arieti Taxis & Tours Ph. 55-752** in the Muri Beach area, **Doro's Taxi Ph. 52-355** in Avana, **JP Taxis Ph. 55-107** in Arorangi and **Parekura Taxis Ph. 55-870** in Avarua. At NZ$2.50 per kilometer, you can figure about NZ$40.00 for a taxi from Muri Beach to the airport.

Bus Service

There is an excellent bus service on Rarotonga. Buses run around the island at hourly intervals, both clockwise (on the hour) and counterclockwise (on the half hour). Daytime service Monday through Saturday, begins at 7:00 AM and continues to 4:00 PM. The Sunday bus schedule runs from 8:00 AM to 12 Noon and then at 2:00 and 4:00 PM. The bus runs clockwise only on Sunday.

You need just flag down the bus anywhere on the road to catch a ride. Rates are NZ$3.00 to any destination and you can purchase a pass for ten rides for NZ$20.00 direct from the bus driver. Children ride for a reduced fare of NZ$1.50.

If you hop the bus in Avarua, you can circumnavigate the entire island for $3.00. The buses are clean and the drivers all seem to possess a good sense of humor. This is also a good chance to meet locals as many use the buses. Below is the bus schedule

The night buses, run hourly starting at 6:00 PM and continuing until 11:00 PM on Monday through Thursday, they leave on the hour in a clockwise direction only. The Friday night schedule is hourly from 6:00 PM until 10:00 PM, with a Midnight and 2:00 AM bus to take home the final revelers from the bars. Saturday is a bit different, as the bars close at midnight (per law), hourly buses run from 6 to 11:00 PM. There are **No Night Buses on Sunday.**

Day Time Schedule

Clockwise		Counterclockwise	
00	Cook's Corner	25	Cook's Corner
02	Paradise Inn	27	Market Place
04	Club Raro	28	CITC Supermarket
05	KiiKii Motel	30	RSA/Airport
08	Ariana Bungalows	32	CTC Supermarket
10	Mataverra Village Traders	34	Orchid Motel
11	Avana Condos	35	Tiare Village
13	Aroko Bungalows	37	Golf Club
14	Sokala Villas Muri Beach Club Resort	39	Oasis/Sunset Resort
15	Pacific Resort	40	Edgewater Resort
16	Muri Beach/Sailing Club Muri Beachcomber	41	Crown Beach Resort
17	Vara's Beach House	42	Manuia Beach
18	Ara Mango/Muri Beach Resort	43	Are Renga Motel
20	Little Polynesian	45	Castaway Beach Bungalows
21	Moana Sands	46	Sunhaven/Rarotongan Backpackers
25	Palm Grove	47	Puaikura Reef Lodge
26	Waterfall	47	Aroa's Beachside Inn
27	Daydreamer/Piri's Place	48	Backpackers International
30	Rarotongan Resort	49	Lagoon Lodges
31	Lagoon Lodges	50	Rarotongan Resort

Clockwise		Counterclockwise	
32	Backpackers International	53	Dadreamer/Piri's Place
33	Puaikura Reef Lodge Aroa's Beachside Inn	54	Waterfall
34	Sunhaven/Rarotongan Backpackers	55	Palm Grove
35	Castaway Beach Bungalows	00	Moana Sands
36	Cook Island Lodges	01	Little Polynesian
37	Are Renga Motel	02	Are Mango/Muri Beach Resort
38	Manuia Beach Hotel	03	Muri Beachcomber/Vara's
39	Crown Beach Resort	05	Pacific Resort
40	Edgewater Resort	06	Sokala Villas
41	Sunset Resort	07	Aroko Bungalows
42	Oasis	09	Avana Condos
43	Golf Club	10	Sunrise Beach Motel
46	RSA/Airport	12	Matavera Village Traders
47	CTC Supermarket	14	Ariana Bungalows
48	Market Place	15	Kiikii Motel
50	Cook's Corner	16	Club Raro
		18	Paradise Inn
		20	Cook's Corner

Night Bus Schedule

Clockwise	
00	Cook's Corner/Banana Court
01	Trader Jack's/Raro Fried Chicken
02	Waterfront Cafe/Staircase Whatever Bar
03	Japanese Sushi/Portofino
04	Mac's Place Tamaring House
05	Club Raro
06	Super Brown Takeaways
14	Flame Tree
15	Pacific Resort

Clockwise	
16	Sails Restaurant
17	Vara's Beach House
19	Little Polynesian
20	Moana Sands
24	Palm Grove
25	Wigmore's Superstore
26	Vaima Restaurant
27	Daydreamer/Piri's
30	Rarotongan Resort
31	Kaena Restaurant
32	Lagoon Lodges
33	Puaikura Reef Lodges
34	International Backpackers
36	Castaway Villas
37	Lime Cafe
38	Manuia Beach Hotel
39	Windjammer Restaurant
40	Edgewater/Spag House
40	Tumunu
42	Roadhouse
43	Alberto's Steakhouse
45	RSA/Airport
48	Market Place
48	Palace Takeaways/SFC Ravis Restaurant
50	Cook's Corner/Moe-Jo's/Hideaway Bar

Bicycle, Motorbike or Car Rentals

There are a number of places to rent bicycles and motorbikes on the island. Bicycles go for around NZ$8.00 per day and motorbikes go for about NZ$15.00 per day. Slightly better rates can be negotiated on weekly rates. I found the best pricing from **Rarotonga Rentals Ph. 22-326,** they have a location in Avarua and one across the street from the airport. I prefer a motorbike in lieu of a car, but they have bikes, motorbikes and cars available. In addition you can try **Polynesian Bike Hire Ltd. Ph. 20-895**, Polynesian has four locations throughout the island and also offer bikes, motorbikes and cars. The same goes for **Island Car & Bike Hire Ph. 22-632**. There is a local franchise of **Budget Rent A Car Ph. 20-895** that has five locations and they have four-day packages at reasonable rates. I found it best to call around and get a price quote from all four, as most everyone seems to advertise the best prices in town.

April 12th, 2008 was declared "H Day" in Rarotonga, which was to become the day that helmets, became mandatory on the Island. Two days before the law was to take effect, Prime Minister Jim Marurai and his cabinet rescinded the law, as long as you are riding your scooter at a maximum of 40 km. per hour or less. At the time this is written there are a variety of angry shopkeepers on Rarotonga, with a substantial stock of helmets and distaste for politicians. The final chapter on the helmet saga is still to be written, such is the politics of small island nations. In the mean time, you can get a hell of a deal on a helmet in Rarotonga. The law was only intended for Rarotonga; the outer islands were not affected, including the Prime Minister's home island of Mangaia.

Things To Do

There are a wide variety of activities on Rarotonga. Some visitors are up each morning and off to experience the many sightseeing and recreation opportunities available, while others adopt a leisurely pace and spend their days lounging on the deck or floating about the lagoon. Below I list my favorites in order of preference. Use this as a guide; depending on your particular interests and tastes, you may want to partake in all or none of the list. Remember, it is your vacation; enjoy it in the way you see fit. To my thinking all activities are reasonably priced and offer value to the traveler.

The **day trip to Aitutaki** heads my list, for visitors to Rarotonga, who are not otherwise planning to visit this island. Aitutaki is less than an hour away by plane and is said by many to be the Pacific's most beautiful atoll. The scenery is quite different from volcanic Rarotonga; the island has a very large lagoon with many small islands circling the perimeter. Your day trip includes a guided tour of the island including a cruise and lunch on a *motu* the Maori word for small inlet. The tour operator will provide towels and snorkeling gear, so you need not bring this along on the plane. The cost includes transfers to and from your hotel. Flights departs at 8:00 A.M. and return at 7:30 P.M. You can make arrangements at your hotel tour desk, direct from **Air Rarotonga Ph. 22-888** or use **Jetsave Travel Ph. 27-707**. The cost at NZ$449.00 for adults and NZ$295.00 for children 2-11 is rather steep, but I can't imagine having come all the way from the states and not visiting this South Pacific treasure. Keep an eye out for discounted trips while shopping in Avarua, as these are often available in off peak season.

Island Nights

This is the second on my list of compulsorily activities during your stay on Rarotonga. It should be number one if you are only going to be on the island for a brief stay and will not be able to

take the day trip to Aitutaki. The Cook Islanders are known throughout Polynesia for their dancing and there are several dance troops on the islands that perform at "island night" shows in various locations.

The night begins with an *Umukai*, the traditional Polynesian feast. A hole is dug in the ground, and a fire is started, then the *umu* is lined with rocks. Once the fire dies down, green banana stalks and leaves are placed in the hole to create a liner, which by now is steaming away. The food or *kai* is then placed in the earthen oven and additional layers of banana or hibiscus leaves are placed on top with a covering of dirt. The *kai*, typically a pig or fish, along with various side dishes is then left to steam in its own juices for a couple of hours at which point you have created the Polynesian equivalent of "fast food".

Once the food is consumed, the dancing or *kaiori* begins. The dancers, in traditional costumes, put on an hour of shaking, swaying and knee knocking fever, the likes of which you have never seen. The highlight arrives when visitors are randomly picked from the crowd to attempt the native dances. The cost of the show and dinners vary; listed below is the current chart of island nights on Rarotonga. Keep in mind that the quality of the meals and ambiance will vary from location to location. Since there are many dance troops on the island, I'll have to plead the Fifth Amendment on the quality of the singing and dancing; those male dancers are not to be angered!

Island Night Schedule

Day	Hotel/ Restaurant	Troop	Dinner/ Show	Show
Mon.	**Pacific Resort Ph. 20-427** Island Night Dinner Plus Show	Te Korero Dance Troupe	NZ65 Child (6-12) NZ$35	N/A
Tues.	**Edgewater Resort Ph. 25-435** Island Night Buffet Plus Show	Taakoka Dance Troupe	NZ$55 Child (6-12) NZ$25	NZ$15
	Crown Beach Resort Ph. 23-953 Island Night Dinner Plus Show	Nukura Dance Troupe	NZ$55 Child (6-12) NZ$15	NZ$10
	Rarotongan Beach Resort Ph 25-800 Island BBQ with fire dance	Tamariki Manuia Group	NZ$55 Child (6-12) Half Price	NZ$25
Wed.	**Rarotongan Beach Resort Ph 25-800** Island Night Buffet Plus Show	Orama Dance Group	NZ$55 Child (6-12) Half price	NZ$25

Day	Hotel/ Restaurant	Troop	Dinner/ Show	Show
Thurs.	**Staircase Restaurant Ph. 22-254** Island Night Dinner Plus Show	Te Manava Troupe	NZ$30 Child (6-12) Half Price	NZ$5.
Fri.	**Pacific Resort Ph. 20-427** Island Night Dinner Plus Show	Tamariki Manuia Group	NZ$55 Child (6-12) NZ$35	N/A
Sat.	**Edgewater Resort Ph. 25-435** Island Night Buffet Plus Show	OramaE Matike Dance Group	NZ$55 Child (6-12)NZ$25	NZ$15
	Rarotongan Beach Resort Ph 25-800 Island Night Buffet Plus Show	E Matriki Dance Troupe	NZ$55.00 Child (6-12) Half Price	NZ$25
	Manuia Beach Hotel Ph. 22-461 Island Night Buffet Plus Show	Manuia Troupe	NZ$50 Child (6-12) Half Price	NZ10

Dinner at all locations starts at 7PM & shows start at about 8:30 PM. There are no island night shows on Sunday, but **Paw Paw Patch (Ph. 27-189)** has a barbeque buffet with string band entertainment, served on the beach in front of the Moana Sands Resort. Call ahead for reservations. Sunday night is grill night at the **Point Restaurant (Ph.23-000)** on the grounds of the new Muri Beach Club Hotel, entertainment is provided by Jake Numanga, on loan between flights at the airport. Tuesday and Saturday nights **Aroa's Beachside Inn (Ph. 22-166)** has sunset barbecues on the beach, featuring local entertainers, these are quite popular so be sure and call ahead to reserve space.

Scuba & Snorkeling

If scuba diving is your passion there are a variety of tour operators available on the island.

Greg Wilson's Cook Island Divers Ph. 22-483 www.cookislanddivers.com E-Mail: gwilson@ci-divers.co.ck has the oldest dive operation on the island. For thirty-five years they have been assisting traveling divers and can offer a variety of certifications from a host of international diving organizations. Cook Island Divers has the largest dive certification program in the Asia/pacific region, excluding Australia. Their twice-daily dive trips and are equally adapt at handling beginners all the way up to experts. Turn left directly across from the Crown Beach Resort as you head south out of Avarua. If your trip is in the early planning stage you will want to visit their extensive Website.

Pacific Divers Ph. 22-450 Check out their Website, **www.pacificdivers.co.ck.** E-Mail: **dive@pacificdivers.co.ck** They are located in Ngatangiia, on the left across from Muri Beach, just past the Flame Tree Restaurant. Owners Graham and Christina McDonald, like the folks at Cook Island Divers also offer twice daily dive trips. If you are a beginning diver what better location to start at than the pristine waters of Muri Lagoon? One dive in the warm waters of the lagoon will spoil you for life. The water off California will suddenly resemble vegetable soup and that job at Wal-Mart will lose its attraction. They specialize in two tank dives and offer certified PADI open water and advanced open water dive courses.

In the southwest corner of Rarotonga, on Aroa's Beach **The Dive Centre Ph. 20-238 www.thedivecentre-rarotonga.com** E-Mail:info@divecentre-rarotonga.com is located right on the main road.   They are open seven days a week, offering all those dive necessities, two tank dives, PADI certification as well as friendly helpful service. If you want to go snorkeling but left you flippers back on the mainland they will gladly rent you the equipment to snorkel the reef off Aroa's Beach. They seem like good folks, offering storage of gear and free transport, I guess life in Rarotonga has mellowed them.

The islands final accredited diving operation is **Dive Rarotonga**

Ph. 21-873 www.diverarotonga.com
E-Mail: info@diverarotonga.com
 they are located on the beach side of the main road in the black rock area. Just look for the big yellow A-frame building. They specialize in small groups and offer a four to one student to instructor ratio. They advertise small, fun dive groups, like all the rest they will pick you up and deliver you back to your lodging.

Over the years I have visited all four of the operators and I must say they are all quite serious about safety, while still exhibiting that Kiwi sense of adventure. You run into the dive instructors at the local watering holes, young and charming, frequently accompanied by their dive customers. If asked they all swear by whichever firm they dive with, so I am reasonably sure they all do a good job. If you are a serious diver, I suggest you spend time on their websites and find which operator tends to meet your needs. In the clear water of Rarotonga, you really can't go wrong.

Rates are generally in the NZ$70.00 to NZ$80.00 range, with discounts for multiple dives. Use your own equipment or their gear. If you plan on completing your PADI or NAUI certification course, figure on spending four days at a cost of between NZ$350.00 to NZ$400.00. I am told that diving the wreck of the SS Maitai is one of the favorite dives and well worth the trip to the north shore.

If you prefer to dive and snorkel without the aid of an oxygen tank, you may want to try **Reef To See Ph. 22-212. E-Mail: reef2see@oyster.net.ck** They offer guided snorkel trips of Rarotonga's barrier reef and include all the necessary equipment. This is an excellent choice for families and for those of us that find the vast scuba equipment to be claustrophobic. Tours are at 9:00 and 2:00 daily and I find their motto, "we dive the calm side", to be reassuring, especially if you went on the, "pub crawl" the night before. Talk to Terry or Margaret, they know what's under every rock in the lagoon.

Another interesting snorkeling alternative is one of Rarotonga's newest adventure tours, **Poko's Night Snorkeling Ph. 70-404,** which operates Monday through Friday. Poko will pick you up at your hotel, transport you to the beach, where you will receive a safety briefing and be issued your wet suit and gloves for an unforgettable evening of snorkeling with the aid of a powerful flashlight. When you return to the beach, you will partake in a tasty barbeque, while Poko tells island tales of Friday nights at Banana Court

In addition to the organized snorkeling, some of the hotels provide snorkeling equipment free to their guests and the lagoon in front of your hotel can provide hours of exploration possibilities. Stay away from inlets (dark water) as the tide and current can launch you towards Aitutaki if you stray too close. Sharks do inhabit this area of the South Pacific, but a shark attack is extremely rare. Remember that sharks are attracted to blood, and as long as you have not speared a fish or cut yourself on the coral they will have no interest in you. In addition to the free snorkeling equipment that may be available at your hotel, it is possible to rent snorkeling equipment at from **Aqua Sports Shop Ph. 27-350.** They are adjacent to the beach at the Muri lagoon. Another spot to rent snorkeling equipment as well as kayaks is further down Muri lagoon at **Captain Tama's Aquasports Center Ph. 27-350 E-Mail: Weddings@cookislands.co.ck** . In addition to those above, all of the dive shops on the previous page will be happy to rent you equipment.

Sport Fishing

The waters around Rarotonga are home to a variety of finned dinners. Tuna, Mahi-Mahi (Dolphin Fish), Wahoo and Marlin all frequent the sea off the Cook Islands. There are a variety of marine charters operating out of Rarotonga. All of the local Captains claim to know where the big ones are located, but then again, it has been my experience, that there are no bigger liars than fishermen. The marlin season runs from November to March, but most other species call the island home year-round. Inquire as to the disposition of any fish you catch, as some charter operators keep the fish, some distribute them to each paying customer, some sell your fish back to you. Better to enquire prior to booking, just in case you land your Ahi dinner and find out the captain will be eating your dinner instead of you. Cost for a five hour charter range from NZ$80.00 to NZ$100.00

Akura Charters Ph. 54-355 E-Mail: fish@akura.co.ck may be your choice if you prefer a little more stability at sea. At fifty feet, their ship is the largest of the sport fishing fleet on Rarotonga and they offer game fishing for up eight persons. Their fishing trips originate out of the harbor in Avatiu and typically run five to six hours. The skipper Chris Musselle has lived in the Cook Islands for the past thirty-eight years and personally guarantees a good time by all who step aboard the *Akura*. The boat is also available for sightseeing, champagne cocktail cruises or inter-islands charters to Aitutaki. **Fisher's Fishin' Tours Ph. 23-356 E-Mail: bafisher@oyster.net.ck** offers daily trips on their 26 foot, *"Corey Anne"* catamaran. Their ad in Jason's, **Cook Islands what's on**, shows three mates holding up three varieties of the catch of the day, although the blonde with her hands on her hips might be a better catch. Captain Fisher believes in the fish shared policy and has a side business in black pearl jewelry.

Hook Fishing Charters Ph. 54-475 operates a twenty-six foot motorized cruiser in the waters off Avitiu harbor. **Pacific Marine Charters Ph. 21-237 www.pacificmarinecharters.co.ck E-Mail: pacmarine@cookislands.co.ck** operates a daily charter boat out of Avatiu Harbor. Wayne and first mate Jenny operate a fully equipped thirty-one foot sport fisher with (get this ladies) a flush toilet. Aboard the "Reel Time' the fish stays with the boat, but if the catch is substantial, they'll supply you with enough for dinner.

Seafari Charters Ph. 55-096 www.seafari.co.ck E-Mail: greg@seafari.co.ck is another long time charter operator fishing out of the Avatiu Harbor. The *Seafari* is a Canadian built thirty-four foot cruiser and is skippered by local skipper Mata, better known as Sunshine to the local fisherman. The five-hour charter includes lunch, ice water and juice; you bring the beer and the fishing talent. Seafari can handle groups of one to twelve people.

There are a host of other small operators on the island. You may want to check in at the **Cook Islands Game Fishing Club Ph. 21-419** just east of Avarua on the ocean side of the main road. As the name implies there is a host of fishermen that hang out at the bar, shoot pool and discuss the big one that got away. Pull up a stool and introduce yourself, these old salts can help you find a guide and boat.

Island Sea Cruises

If fishing is too much work and you prefer a cruise around the island try contacting Gene or Alberto at **Paradise Sailing Ph. 23-577 www.paradise-sailing.co.ck E-Mail: info@paradise-**

sailing.co.ck Take a trip aboard the 38' trimaran *Hotel California*. Let me know if you see Gilligan or the Captain on this three-hour cruise. As I recall, Gilligan's trip didn't include snorkel equipment, (snorkeling optional), food and drinks but this trip includes all that. Becoming shipwrecked involves additional charges not included in the normal fare. Assuming you opt for the standard cruise you will leave at 1:00 and return at 4:00. The *Hotel California* is available for whatever additional charter options you may have in mind, just give Gene or Alberto a call. I have only one-question guys; does Don Henley know you are using his song title? I hear he is a bit touchy about use of his almighty lyrics. Rates for the afternoon sailing is Adult/Child NZ$75.00/NZ$35, which includes fresh snacks and drinks. I know some of the Americans out there can down a substantial sum of Margaritas, in three hours and a healthy Kiwi can certainly down a dozen Steinlagers during the cruise, perhaps that is why the cost is a little on the high side. A warning, too many libations on a rocky platform can lead to the art of chumming on the way home.

Reef Walking

The lagoon that circles the island offers many varieties of shellfish, coral, crabs, reef fish, starfish and sea urchins. If you don't have a pair of specifically designed reef walkers, use an old pair of sneakers. Don't try reef walking with just a pair of thongs, the coral is sharp and coral cuts take a long time to heal. Keep in mind coral is a living organism, so step carefully on your walk. There is no need to travel to a far off beach; the lagoon in front of your hotel may offer the best reef walking on the island, just go get your feet wet.

Hiking

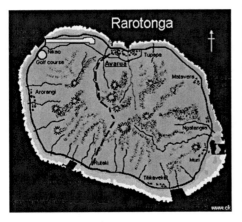

There are many tracks and trails on Rarotonga that offer both the casual and experienced hiker an opportunity to view the rugged interior of the island. The **cross-island trek** is probably the most popular on the island. While the hike is only about seven kilometers, figure to take three to four hours to complete the hike, it takes you in close proximity of the needle, Rarotonga's most prominent mountain peak, known locally as *Te Rua Manga,* which is Maori for, you guessed it, "the needle". Wear serious shoes for the hike and bring along sufficient water. Don't forget your insect repellant, as you will need it almost as much as that water.

To reach the starting point of the cross-island trek you can take the island bus to the Avatiu harbor and follow the road that leads inland behind the Dockside Cafe. Just stay on this road and follow the signs up the Avitiu Valley past the parking area following the footpath. The path is fairly level for the first ten minutes then it crosses a stream and begins the climb to the needle, which takes about forty-five minutes and will wear you out. When you reach the top you will come to a T-intersection and the path to the right is a ten-minute trip to the base of the needle, which can be climbed, but only by very serious rock climbers. The rest of us, after viewing the needle will retrace our path back towards the T-intersection, but just before you reach the T, branch off to the right and follow the white plastic cable down the hill until you reach the stream, at which point the trail follows the stream down to a fern covered valley, where the trail branches off to the right and leads down to Wigmore's Waterfall. Take a dip in the cool water below the fall, but remember to reapply insect repellant before beginning the fifteen-minute walk down to the coast road. Flag down the island bus and it will take you back to your car or hotel, where you can go for a swim or take a nap to recover from the hike which is a lot harder to accomplish than what you thought; or at least that is what I have been told.

Another popular hike is known as **Raemaru Hike** and offers excellent views of the west coast of Rarotonga and the Muriavai Valley. This hike, like the cross-island hike, is quite strenuous and should only be attempted by those in relatively good health. If you take the island bus, get off just south of the CICC Church at the south end of Arorangi Village. If you tell the bus driver that you are going on the Raemaru Hike, he will tell you where to get off the bus. You will walk up Akaoa Road about a hundred yards to *Ara Matua*, the old island road. When you come to the road, you will turn right and continue south where there will be a small dirt road almost immediately on your left. Follow this road up the hill and look for a dirt track up the hill. Once you follow this path you will come to some terraces and the remains of an old pineapple orchard, bear left at the pineapple orchard and follow the switchback path up the north side of Raemaru to the ridgeline. From here a narrow trail leads to the summit and the view of the valley below. Return the way you came and when you get back to the coast road you can flag down the bus to get back to your accommodation and happy hour.

The two hikes listed above are the most popular and are fairly serious hiking trips. If you are planning either of the hikes above and would prefer to take along a guide, there are various tour operators that can provide a guide. For the cross-island trek contact **Reef & Rainforest Guiders Ph. 22-407 E-Mail: tiutematangi@yahoo.com** The venerable and quite popular **Pa Ph. 21-079** leads groups most every day of the week, see his listing under tours in this section of the book.

For more gentle hikes try hiking up the Turangi, Avana or Avatiu Valley's or along the miles of shoreline that surround the island. For more detailed information and maps, pick up a copy of *Rarotonga's Mountain Tracks and Plants,* or *Rarotonga's Cross-Island Walk.* Both of these booklets are available at Bounty Books in Avarua, and both are excellent and give detailed information about all of the natural features, plants and animals you will encounter during your hikes in the interior of the island. If you are less adventurous and would prefer a guide for your hike, see Pa's Mountain Treks listed under guided tours a little further back in this chapter.

Surfing

That's right dude, they got surfin' on Rarotonga. While hardly World Class, you will see a number of surfers and boogie boarders around the harbor inlet in Avarua when the surf is up. Another popular surfing spot is outside the Ngatangiia passage on the southeast side of the island. Check in at **Nick's Surf**

Shop Ph. 26-240 in Tuapa to check out the latest surf wear and find out where to catch that wild surf.

Golf

If surfing sounds a bit to intensive, you are welcome to try your luck at Rarotonga's nine-hole golf course. While the course does not rank anywhere near Hawaii's Kapalua and was not designed by Greg Norman, it has it's own charm. The course is situated amongst the island's radio towers and local rules allow you to take a shot over without penalty if you hit the guide wires or the tower itself. Play at your own risk, what the locals lack in talent, they make up for by swinging harder. The average Maori creates as much club head speed as Tiger Woods, the only question is will he make contact with the ball, and if so, will it land on the island. I especially enjoyed the nineteenth hole, reasonably priced drinks to drown your sorrows. The golf course is on the left hand side of the main road south of Avarua in the Black Rick area of Rarotonga. The course is open 8 AM to 4 PM, with the bar open to mid evening. Green Fees are NZ$ 15.00 with club rental the same. The course is reseved for members on Saturday and closed on Sunday.

Whale Watching

Most dive and sportfishing operators, including **Pacific Divers** (see scuba diving) and **Paradise Sailing** (island sea cruises) offer whale-watching trips in season. The humpbacked whale call Rarotonga home from July to October. Many times they can be seen breaching just off the reef during these months.

Tours

There are a wide variety of tours on the Island of Rarotonga, not including the day trip to Aitutaki, at the top of this list of things to do on Rarotonga. The tours range from active to passive and all show a unique facet of Island beauty or culture that is totally unique to the Cook Islands. So pick and choose the ones that interest you and above all have a great time.

Pa Teuruaa is somewhat of an institution on the island, his **Pa's Mountain Trek Ph. 21-079** tours come in two varieties his cross-island *trek* takes five hours and is not for the casual hiker. It winds up through the valley just inland from Avatiu, past *The Needle,* as Tia Rua Manga is known and ends on the other side of the island near the village of Vaimaangra. Pa has a gentle way about him, his blond dreadlocks surround a sincere  smile and locally he is as well known for his knowledge of local medicine as he is for his guided tours.

You may want to familiarize yourself with the island by taking a round island tour; **Raro Tours Ph.25-324** offers this service Monday through Friday, in their air-conditioned buses. The tour lasts for three and one half hours and the cost is NZ$45.00. When you return from the tour you will have picked up a bit of the island history and customs, visited some of the interesting buildings and churches of the island all from the air conditioned comfort of a tour bus.

"Never park under the coconut tree and never lie", says Piri Puruto in his legend of the pacific show, "Just live with love, peace and harmony and you have captured the essence of the Cook Islands", Sage advise from the star of this one-man show. Shows are five days a week Monday through Friday and Thursday's show features the traditional Umukai Feast. Reservations are essential; phone **Piri The Legend of the Pacific Ph.20-309** let it ring for a while, for he may be up in a coconut tree when you call.

Find out about Cook Island Culture, History, and Geography on the, **Raro Mountain Safari Tour Ph. 23-629.** **www.rarosafaritours.co.ck** **E-Mail:** **sambo@earosafaritours.co.ck** Wisecracking Dennis "Black Magic" Heather was my driver and guide on the tour and there was nothing of the islands past, present or future that Dennis didn't know or have an opinion on. The former island bus driver has spent the last 3-1/2 years going, "up and down the island", as opposed to round and round the island in his bus. Dennis' knowledge on all island subjects made  the trip a joy and I enjoyed visiting portions of the island that are inaccessible by any other means. The safari tours three Land Rovers are remarkably stable and easy riding as you climb the backcountry of Rarotonga. This is a trip that I highly recommend, especially for families, just tell Dennis I sent you and you want to feel that, "Cook Islands massage". The price is NZ$60.00 for an adult, half price for children 6-11, and children under 6 years old are free. The price includes pick up and delivery from your hotel and light tropical refreshments. A second safari type tour operator entered the market recently, **Tangaroa Tours, Ph. 22-200 www.tangaroa4x4.co.ck E-Mail: joinus@tangaroa4x4.co.ck** offers much the same as the safari tour, but throws in the preparation of an *umu,* (traditional earth oven) for groups of six or more. Tours are Monday thru Friday from 9:00 to 12:30 and Sunday 12:00 Noon to 3:30 PM. Adults are NZ$60.00, Children 6-11 are half price and the tour includes your *umukai* lunch and all transfers. Tangaroa, being the benevolent ruler, will accept all major credit cards.

On my first trip to Rarotonga in 1994 I learned of Raymond Pirangi's quest to resurrect the remains of the old historical village of Maungaroa, ancestral home of the island's Tinomana tribe in the highlands above Arorangi. When I visited the Cook Islands to research the first edition of this book in 2003, I was told that Raymond was still at it, but no completion date was forthcoming. At that point I dismissed the project as akin to the Sheraton Hotel, a never-ending saga. I must say, unlike the Sheraton Hotel, Raymond Pirangi's dream has become a reality. **Highland Paradise (Ph. 21-924) www.highlandparadise.co.ck E-Mail: highland@oyster.net.ck** It is now possible to visit this 205 acre ancient sacred site with over 12 acres of tropical gardens, to visit a pre-Christian village reclaimed from the tropical forest. Tours run Monday thru Saturday at 10:00 AM and 2:00 PM, with a special sunset tour at 5:00 PM, which includes an *umu* (earth oven) meal. Costs of the tour are NZ$50.00 for adults, children 6-12 are half price and children under six are prepared in the *umu.* I was only kidding! Children under 6 are free. Transfers are NZ$5.00 each way, bringing you up to what appears to be the going rate for tours NZ$60.00. Call ahead for reservations on this worthwhile trip into a pre-Christianity Rarotonga. Elements of the now closed Cultural Village Tour have been moved to the Highlands site and many of the demonstrations are available as part of this tour.

The **Takitumu Nature Cobservation Area Guided Tour, (Ph. 29-906) E-Mail: kakerori@tca.co.ck** is an excellent way for visitors to get a first hand look at operations to conserve the native Rarotongan flycatcher (Kakerori) and their habitat. The conservation area established in 1996 is a community based protected area established by the traditional landowners to protect the birds. The two-hour guided tour is mostly a gentle walk, with some uneven terrain. As with any inland tour on Rarotonga, I recommend that you bring along insect repellant to ward off any mosquitos. Birdwatchers will have a chance to see a variety of island species and your guide will explain the medicinal powers of several plants along the trail. The tour costs NZ$45.00 for adults and NZ$27.00 for children and includes lunch. All proceeds are used to ensure the survial of the endangered Rarotonga flycatcher. A worthy cause and a worthwhile tour.

Once you have your fill of island culture, you may be searching for the tour that is, "No 1 under the sun in Rarotonga". **Captain Tama's Lagoon Cruises Ph. 27-350** is another long time favorite of visitors. The captain's cruise leaves Monday through Saturday at 11:00 and returns at 3:30, so don't forget your sunscreen. The tour includes a trip on a glass bottomed catamaran to one of the four *motus* in Muri Lagoon, where you will be served a "sumptuous barbecued fish lunch" and forced to snorkel the day away amongst giant clams, sea turtles and a demonstration black pearl farm. Tama and his crew have been doing this for many years, but have not lost their charm and good humor. Captain Tama's is located next to the sailing club; call ahead for reservations. The cost is NZ$50.00 for adults and NZ$25.00 for children 6-11 and the cost includes transfers to and from your accommodation. In addition to the tours, Captain Tama's Aquasports has windsurfers and kayaks for rent. This will give you a chance to finish your sunburn. **Adventure Hire Ltd (Ph. 24-123)** **www.adventurehire.co.ck** **E-Mail: info@adventurehire.co.ck** rents a variety of water-based paraphernalia from Snorkeling sets for a daily rate of (NZ$10) to single/double kayaks at (NZ$15/$25) for 3 hours. Going native? Rent a two-person outrigger for (NZ$25) for three hours, or if your arms are tired try a foot-powered cruzicat for the same rate. You can even rent a solar powered boat for NZ$20.00 per hour. If you want to dry off from the lagoon, rent an Apollo mountain bike for (NZ$13) per day or a tandem bike for (NZ$21). There are two locations to choose from, across from the beach at Kavera Beach or on the grounds of the Muri Beach Club Hotel

There are a couple of newer tours on the island, one of which is **Cook Islands Kayak Adventure Tours Ph. 25-359** which offers daily and multi day kayak tours of the island. The adventurous traveler will spend a full day exploring the waters of Rarotonga on this guided tour. Group size is limited to a maximum of eight, so call ahead for booking information. **Bluewater Adventures Ltd. Ph. 71-443** offers a variety of water-based activities. My favorite is night *Maroro* fishing, which combines the art of butterfly catching with the skill of fishing. This can be a great family adventure, blasting around just outside the reef, chasing the tiny silver bullets that soar in and out of your boat mounted spotlight. I'm sure you can picture the endless laughter that is a distinct possibility of this endeavor. Traditional daytime sport fishing is also available as are charters to surfing spots and whale watching in season. Their open charters can be tailored to your needs, wakeboarding, tubing or just a day on the water, contact the staff to customize a Bluewater Adventure of your own.

Can you fly? Well if you book a tour with **Adventure Microflight Ph. 55-311** you will likely soar to new heights. Forgive me, for I am running low on clever openings and that is the best I could concoct. When you complete your trial flight with your qualified pilot/instructor you will become an official member of Microflight Association. Reasonable health and a spirit of adventure are all that is required. For those under 16 a parent's consent is also a necessity. I couldn't get my mom to let me go, but probably would have flunked the physical anyway. The cost for a one-hour flight is NZ$160.00

Horseback Riding

If you would like to go horseback riding, give a call to **Aroa Pony Treks Ph. 21-415** they are located off the main road near the Rarotongan Resort and offer two-hour rides to Papua waterfall and back. They have both a morning and afternoon trip, call ahead for reservations. The cost is NZ$30.00 per person. My proper British friend John, read this entry and commented, "why do you Americans refer to horse riding as horse*back* riding, where else would you ride a horse but on his back"? I never thought about it but the man has a point, doesn't he?

Shopping

Rarotonga's principal city, Avarua has a variety of gift shops,

 clothing stores and jewelry shops, for those interested in spending time away from the lagoon. The South Sea black pearls from Manahiki and Penrhyn are prized possessions throughout the world. In addition to Pearls, the islands of Penrhyn and Rakahanga are noted for their colorful *Rito* hats,

which adorn the local ladies on Sundays. On many of the islands of the Southern Group, the native pandanus is woven into bags; fans and mats and these as well as the local *Pate* drums are available in the arts and crafts stores in Avarua. You may also want to pick up a *pareu* at one of the shops. This colorful length of material is the, multi-purpose garment of the South Pacific; it can be worn in many different ways. Primarily worn by women and children, but don't be surprised to see a few adorning local males.

As they say, buyers beware, this is especially true when purchasing black pearls, and quality and price vary from store to store. Ask around, talk to other travelers, and enquire at the front desk where you are staying. Almost every islander has a cousin or nephew that is selling black pearls for "wholesale" or so they say. The list that follows, does not indicate an endorsement by me, but these sources have been around for a

while, which indicates they offer fair value. **Bergman and Sons Ph. 21-902** in the large building directly behind the main gas station in Avarua. Bergman's has a small shop at the Edgewater, but I suggest the main store in Avarua. **Beachcomber Gallery Ph. 21-939** is on the main road at the north end of town. They also have a small shop at the Rarotongan Beach Resort. You may also want to try **Raina Trading Ltd. Ph. 23-601** in Avarua or the **Perfume Factory Ph. 22-690**. The Perfume Factory, which is a must for any serious shopper, is located on the *Are Matua* on the backside of Avarua and offers a selection of pearls as well as a variety of unique gift items. You will find a selection of *Pareu* at **Tiki's Pareu Ph. 25-237** along with a helpful staff. The popular clothing items are also available at the **Punanga Nui** outdoor market. The Saturday market is the largest with lots of vendors, selling a variety of handcrafts, clothing and souvenir items as well as the fruits and vegetables that you expect at a market. For arts and craft shopping try **Island Craft Ph. 22-009, Treasure Chest Ph. 22-325.** They are both located in Downtown Avarua and offer a wide selection of gift items.

Punanga Nui Outdoor Market

While I suppose Avarua's outdoor market should be part of the shopping section, I consider it to be far more than shopping. First off, the fruits and vegetables are picked that morning and come direct from the tree. In addition the local fisherman bring in the catch of the day and offer it up for sale. Lastly, the local ladies bring down their special food items and sell various deserts and baked goods. While the market is open all days but Sunday, the largest selection is on Saturday. Come early for the best selection and make sure you try a few of the island treats. The Wednesday market has an emphasis on arts and crafts, so if you are looking for something to take home at a bargain price, you may want to come to the market on that day. A trip to the Punanga Nui outdoor market is an enjoyable cultural event and can be measured in far more than whatever fruits or vegetables you may purchase.

Where To Stay On Rarotonga

The lodging options are numerous on Rarotonga, from backpacker's hostels up to and including fine boutique hotels. Americans will find no destination resorts of the type found on other South Pacific Islands, and the locals just like it that way. No casinos or flashy high rise accommodations on Rarotonga, but instead there are numerous smaller more intimate inns and clustered villas as well as self contained cottages. Much of the island's accommodations include a refrigerator and a kitchenette, to allow the visitor to prepare some of their own meals. Keep in mind that restaurants are scattered throughout the island, so besides the cost savings, having your own kitchen will save you a lot of time in "rush hour" Rarotonga traffic.

I have attempted to list most every accommodation on the island with more than four units, in an attempt to provide as many choices to the reader as I can. In each category I list my favorites, which are highly subjective and subject to my own personal standards. By no means limit yourself to these choices, and if you discover a personal favorite that is not on this list, drop me a line and I will consider it for the next edition of this guide. By the same token if a hotel listed below does not meet your personal standards, write me about it and they may be dropped from the list.

While lodging is spread out throughout the island, much of it is centered on Muri Beach and the Muri Lagoon and the west facing villages of Arorangi and Black Rock. The main town is Avarua, but there is little in the way of accommodations in this town. Since it is only 31 kilometers around Rarotonga on the *Ara Tapu* or main road, there is little danger of being isolated from any point on the island. The hourly island bus service connects the island and offers low cost service to all points. Nearly all lodging is located within easy walking distance of the bus route, so feel free to locate anywhere on the island.

A word about the Cook Island's lodging code may help you in making your selection. The statement, **self-contained** indicates that the room has basic cooking capabilities, in other words pots, pans, dishes and utensils. Most include a toaster and coffeemaker and some even have a microwave. In the listings below, you will see the terms, **standard**, indicating a basic unit, **deluxe** is the next step up which can mean you get a microwave or it is a better unit than whatever they call standard. **Superior**, as the name indicates is a more desirable larger or well-situated unit, usually the best accommodation the lodging has available. You will hear the term, **garden view**, which indicates you are not facing the ocean or lagoon and are instead behind the beach or lagoon front units. **Beachfront or lagoon front** indicates that you have an unobstructed view in close proximity of the mentioned attraction. Be careful of partial Ocean or lagoon views, these can be through a tree or standing on you tip toes on the deck. Always better to take a look first if you can to see just how partial the view is. The term **bungalow** and **villa** are used almost interchangeably in the islands. Both indicate a separate building and most are individual but sometimes there are two units in a bungalow or villa. Be careful of shared decks, in case you are on your honeymoon and share a deck with a family with three kids. I think you get the picture. I think we all understand the term **dormitory** and you will see it used when discussing budget and backpackers accommodations. Dormitory rooms can have up to twelve beds in a room and they may even be bunk beds, these accommodations are best left to the young travelers who are traveling on a shoestring budget. **Shared Bath**, is a term you will see in budget accommodations and indicates that you share a bath with other guests. This can be a bit inconvenient at times but as long as the door locks it is not a major inconvenience. Be careful of lodging that requires you to visit an outdoors toilet, which is a major inconvenience for those of us with weak bladders. You will see the term **Resort** as part of a listing, this indicates that the lodging has a restaurant on site and is not necessarily what we would call a resort back in the United States. Curiously the term **Motel** indicates a higher standard than what we would expect being from the United States. The term is tied to the New Zealand designation of motel and may indicate a better lodging than what you would expect.

I want to touch on early departure and late arrival charges, or vice versa, as most flights to and from the Cook Islands arrive at ungodly hours and depart in the middle of the night. There is no clear policy on what and when you are charged and everyone and every accommodation handles it differently.

If you arrive at 4:30 A.M. as westbound passengers from Los Angeles do, expect to pay for the night before, as the room will have to be vacant in order for you to collapse in it when you get there at 5:30 A.M. This is pretty clear-cut and seems fair; now on to departures. If check out time is 10:00 A.M. and you are not supposed to be at the airport until 9:00 P.M. you are left without a room for nearly twelve hours. Some charge an extra day to be able to use the room, some charge a reduced rate for a partial day and others, dependent upon occupancy will charge you nothing. My suggestion is to bring up the subject a couple days before your departure so that you can see what your options are. Most all will store your bags at no cost until you leave and, assuming you have not been a total ass during your stay, you can probably work out a mutually beneficial financial arrangement for this part of a day. Detailed Rarotonga Accommodation information can be found below. Listed below are all of the major lodgings, with a few smaller places that I have thrown in. Since the publication of the original guide, it seems as though everyone on Rarotonga has a bungalow or two on the beach and is renting them out for income. Some are accredited by the tourism board, some are not, be careful when renting from private parties, ask for references from previous renters, or deal with a local real estate broker who specializes in rentals. One suggestion for people looking for long-term accommodations is to place an ad in the Cook Island News or check the ads upon your arrival on the island. The days of the NZ$125.00 a week bungalow on the beach are long gone, but bargains can be found from time to time. For accommodation information on the outer islands, consult the chapter on each individual island under **Places To Stay.**

Accommodations Rarotonga

Expensive

**Pacific Resort, Ph. (682) 20-427, Fax (682) 21-427,
P.O. Box 790, Rarotonga Cook Islands
Website: www.pacificresort.com
E-mail: rarotonga@pacificresort.co.ck**

If upper-end accommodations were your goal, this would be my suggestion. The Pacific Resort is located on beautiful Muri Beach. Each of the 54 self-contained units is spread throughout the site amongst native plants and flowers as if in a traditional Rarotongan village. The original developer is said to have surveyed every inch of the property prior to designing the hotel. He then built a plywood scale model with every tree located on the site shown on the plywood. Only then did he "cookie cutter" buildings, placing them so as to cause the least disturbance to the site. This attention to detail is evidenced in the resort. Recent changes, have centered around guest services and the cyclones of 2005 caused cosmetic damage to some beachfront units and the loss of a few trees, Hopefully future developers will show the respect for the environment that the Pacific Resort has shown here and at their sister location on Aitutaki. The on-site Sandals Restaurant serves a full range of breakfast, lunch and dinner items in cozy pleasant surroundings. The lagoon-side Barefoot Bar appears to be fitted to the surroundings, with a tree growing right up through the roof. Hot and cold sandwiches are available for lunch on the patio or at the bar and fish and chips will seldom taste as good as they do in these surroundings. Prices begin at NZ$300 single/double, add NZ$50.00 for triple for the 36 one-bedroom garden units, and add NZ$95.00 if you want one with air conditioning. Two-bedroom garden units, of which there are 8 are NZ$360.00 single/double, add NZ$50.00 for a third or fourth person. One bedroom beachfront units with air conditioning are NZ$550 single/double with a similar charge for a third person. Two Bedroom garden villas, with air conditioning are NZ$655.00 for single/double and add NZ$70.00 each for a third, fourth or fifth person. Two bedroom lagoon villas are NZ$850.00 for single/double, add NZ$70.00 for a third, fourth or fifth person. To round it out, an air-conditioned, two bedroom beachfront villa goes for $1,150.00, and like the other types add NZ$70.00 for that third, fourth and fifth person. All units feature a patio with table, chairs and lounges. Kids under 12 are free as long as they bring along their parents and sleep in their room. Use of snorkeling and kayaks is included in room charge. The beachfront units were completely remodeled two years ago and updated. The Pacific Resort features island night dinner with traditional singing and dancing on Monday and Friday nights. (See Island Night Chart)

Rarotongan Beach Resort, Ph. (682) 20-427, Fax (682) 25-799, P.O. Box 103, Rarotonga, <u>Cook Islands</u>
Website: <u>www.Rarotongan.co.ck</u>
E-mail: <u>info@rarotongan.co.ck</u>

The original high end resort on the island and still favored by many that seek this type of accommodation. This 151-room resort has been in operation since 1977, shortly after completion of the International Airport. The hotel was completely remodeled in 1997 and offers some of the finest accommodations to be found in the South Pacific. Each room is air-conditioned and scattered in one and two-story buildings. The resort has handicapped accessible rooms, which are rare in the South

Pacific. Children under 16 can stay free, but you know you have to bring your parents along and stay in their room. The resort has all the frills one would expect, pool, water sports and tennis, in addition sport fishing and island tours can be arranged by just contacting the desk. The prices start at NZ$360 single/double, with a triple going for NZ$435, prices include full breakfast. At the Rarotongan kids stay and play (and at times eat) for free. Check the Website for specials for kids under 12, and as they say, some restrictions apply, but Moko's kids club is an ongoing program and allows kids to dump their parents and play in their own special area. An island night buffet with traditional Maori singing and dancing is featured on Wednesday and Saturday nights. The cost of the meal and show is extra. (See Island Night Chart)

Crown Beach Resort, Ph. (682) 23-953, Fax (682) 23-951
P.O. Box 47, Rarotonga, <u>Cook Islands</u>
Website: <u>www.crownbeach.com</u>
E-mail: <u>info@crownbeach.com</u>

Coming Out Of Shoot #2 On A Bull Named Crown Point Is Rondo! OK, so I couldn't pass up the Rodeo analogy, but with a name like Rondo, I couldn't help but picture a cowboy on a Brahma bull. Although this Idaho cattle farmer may have turned in his chaps and spurs for a flowered shirt and flip flops, the man is a "hands on" operator and the transformation that has taken place since Rondo took over the reigns at Crown Point Resort is nothing short of astonishing. Rondo Perkins secured controlling ownership of Crown Point Resort in 2005, shortly before a string of five Cyclones hit Rarotonga, an occurrence that was unheard of in the islands history. With substantial damage to the resort, the new owner dug his heels in and fought back like the, well, like a cattle rancher does when Mother Nature deals you a bad hand. In his sixties, Rondo was never one to run from a fight and turned his efforts into creating a first class resort. Three years after the last cyclone, the resort is going through the final stages of its transition. Two first-class restaurants serve the revamped 36 units that grace the point. Stone walkways lead to brand new pool courtyard suites, with fixtures and furnishings that are of the finest quality available. Spacious showers sport stone and marble, while kitchenettes feature stainless steel microwaves and refrigerators built in to the casework.

Rondo introduced me to the staff at Crown Point, pointing out that he hired only Cook Islanders, proud of the many family members that worked in various jobs on site. We retired to the relaxed patio of the Ocean's Restaurant, for a tasty lunch break. Rondo shushed the few flies from his plate, jumped up and returned with a battery powered fly exterminator, it's that sort of attention to detail that is one of the hallmarks to a stay at Crown Point. I can tell you one

thing, if cyclones didn't stop him, a few flies don't stand a chance against this cowboy.

Rates start at NZ$500.00 for Garden Villa Suites and Poolside Villa Suites for up to three people, Two-bedroom Villa Suites are NZ$575.00 per night for up to five people. Two Bedroom Poolside Villa Suites are NZ$625.00 for up to five people, with the Beach Front Villa Suites costing NZ$700.00 per night for up to three people. The Courtyard Pool Suites are in essence secluded villas, with private gated enclosures, small intimate pools and covered patios, these rent for $700.00 for up to two guests. Dine in or have your meals served on your own private gazebo by staff.

In a nutshell prepare to be pampered in a first class resort, by a staff that is intent upon fulfilling your every wish. The staff is there to assist you in your preparation to visit, activities on island, dive trips, car rentals, international flights, inter island flights, there is even a wedding planner on staff to assist you, should you wish to tie the knot in paradise. Complimentary tropical breakfast, use of snorkeling equipment, kayaks, fully equipped gym are all included in your room rate.

Edgewater Resort, Ph. (682) 25-435, Fax (682) 25-475, P.O. Box 121, Rarotonga, Cook Islands
Website: www.edgewater.co.ck
E-mail: stay@edgewater.co.ck

The behemoth Edgewater, now nearly 200 units strong, with tennis courts, swimming pool, activities office, car rental agency, beachside bar, and souvenir shops, occupy a few acres behind the Spaghetti House on the west side of the island in the village of Aroroangi. While a little too impersonal for my tastes, the Edgewater has long been the choice for consolidators hawking "package tours" to the masses worldwide. The hotel has eight three-story buildings; with a pricing structure that changes the closer one wants to be to the ocean. The units are quite nice, with the luxury of air-conditioning, in each room. The beach is not one of the better swimming beaches on the island but the pool and bar are well located facing the reef. Besides the tennis courts, additional activities can be arranged and scooters and cars rented at the activities office. The food at Edgewater is less than spectacular—watch out for that sausage—but there are many good restaurants within walking distance of the Edgewater. The Cook Island bus service stops at the registration area, so you don't even need to walk to the main road to visit Avarua or Muri Beach. On Tuesday and Saturday nights, the Edgewater hosts island night, with an *umukai* buffet and traditional singing and dancing. There is an additional charge for this. (See Island Night Chart) Rates at the Edgewater are NZ$210.00 in the standard garden rooms, the superior garden rooms (closer to beach) are NZ$245.00 with the beachfront rooms at NZ$285.00 per night. The VIP beachfront suites, which are larger and come with Jacuzzi tubs in the baths are NZ$415. All rooms come with a queen size and single bed, but an additional $115 is charged if a third adult (over 12) occupies the room. If you book a standard garden unit and upgrade after you arrive, the cost is less than the rate above, subject to availability. In recent years the Edgewater has added some VIP Deluxe Studio Units (NZ$410.00) and several three-bedroom executive villas (NZ$475.00 to their line up. The three bedroom villas are quite spacious and suitable for three couples or two couples and a child or two.

Sokala Villas, Ph. (682) 29-200, Fax (682) 21-222
P.O. Box 82, Rarotonga, <u>Cook Islands</u>
Website: <u>www.sokalavillas.com</u>
E-mail: <u>villas@sokala.co.ck</u>

Sokala Villas does not fall easily into a particular category, for it offers few of the attributes that characterize high-end accommodations. Yet the setting, amongst coconut palms and fronting the lagoon, sets Sokala apart somewhere between moderate and expensive. Nearly 80% of the bookings at Sokala are from honeymooners, so as you might have guessed children under 12 are not permitted. Sokala is located on Muri Lagoon and five of the seven self contained, one-bedroom villas come equipped with their own swimming pool set in the deck. No two of these excellently appointed villas are the same. Four units are two stories, three of which are single story, all of which front the lagoon; Rates are based upon different categories and amenities, mainly if the unit has a pool. The popular Flame Tree restaurant is next door and there are several other restaurants within walking distance of the villas. Rates vary depending on when you book and pay for your vacation. Check their Website for special early bird and super early bird discounts. Rack rates are NZ$390.00 for a lagoon view one bedroom without pool and NZ$590.00 for a lagoon view one bedroom with a pool.

Beachside units are NZ$690.00 with or without pool. Book ahead if you want a beachside pool unit.

The Navigator is a fairly new two-bedroom beachfront villa. Rates for this two bedroom, beachfront villa are set at NZ$690.00. The villa's first floor is handicap accessible, fully air-conditioned and has it's own pool. This villa represents a bargain for two couples, and is actually next door to Sokala.

Takitumu Villas, Ph. (682) 24-682, Fax. (682) 24-683
PO Box 1031, Rarotonga, <u>Cook Islands</u>
Website: <u>www.royaletakitumu.com</u>
Email: <u>comfort@takitumuvillas.co.ck</u>

Similar in size and amenities to Sokala Villas, Takitumu Villas was inadvertently missed in the original edition of this guidebook. Shame on us! Located in the village of Titikaveka, this intimate and very romantic 10 Unit villa complex is located

within a few steps of the lagoon, rates are NZ$599 for beachfront villas, NZ$460 for lagoon view villas and NZ$545 for the honeymoon villa. Add NZ$75.00 for an extra adult in any villa. All fully self-contained villas are air-conditioned, have thatched roofs, and feature a covered verandah with a view of Titikaveka lagoon. Rates include snorkeling and kayaking equipment as well as "guest only" events and a welcome breakfast basket upon arrival. The staff promises personal service and a caring approach to your stay at their lodging.

86

Airport transfers are not included, but are available at NZ$30.00 return. Children under 12 are not permitted at Takitumu Villas.

Te Vakaroa Villas, Ph. (682) 22-130, Fax (682) 22-136
PO Box, Rarotonga, Cook Islands
Website: www.ck/tevakaroa/index.htm
E-Mail: tevakaroa@villavacations.co.ck

These six new luxury villas are the newest project of Des and Cassy Eggleton, founders of Lagoon Lodges. Designed for the top end visitor to Rarotonga, the one and two bedroom villas feature, modern teak and wicker furnishings, personal Jacuzzis off the master bedrooms, air conditioning and personal wireless Internet. The complex features three one-bedroom villas downstairs and three two-bedroom units upstairs. All units have covered patios and verandahs and there is a large infinity pool that serves the units. The spotless ground feature extensive Natural Island landscaping. While no restaurant is included in the complex, arrangements have been made with neighboring resorts to provide meals delivered to the villas. Rates are NZ$635.00 per night for the one bedroom villas and NZ$695.00 per night for the two bedroom villas. Optional for the two bedroom units is a third person at an additional NZ$60.00. No children under 12 are allowed in the villas

Muri Beach Club Hotel Ph. (682) 23-000 Fax. (682) 23-001
PO Box 3050, Rarotonga, Cook Islands
Website: www.muribeachclubhotel.com
Email: info@muribeachclubhotel.com

This is the new kid on the block, the long time project of owner John Scott, who's original vision was a beach club, but early on realized the premier property deserved far more than a restaurant on Muri lagoon. A decision was made and full-fledged resort was planned. The Scott's family poultry business provided the early financing and progress crept along which fueled the story amongst locals that the hotel was being built one egg at a time. Later additional financing was secured, but many on the island still ask the question, how many eggs were needed to build a resort.

The end result was a full service resort, with 30 beachfront, garden and poolside units within a two-story complex, located at the point of Muri Lagoon. The property lacks much in the way of South Pacific charm, but once the landscaping fills in I am hopeful the hotel will blend a bit better with the surroundings. Room rates are hardly chicken feed, starting at NZ$375.00 single/double for a garden room with two super queen sized beds large enough to accommodate four friendly adults. Premier garden rooms are $425.00, with the same bed configuration. Extra guests in the garden rooms are NZ$50.00 each up to a maximum of four. Superior pool view rooms are NZ$499.00 with a super king sized bed and either a queen or single bed in the room. Deluxe beachfront rooms are a whopping NZ$599.00 and come with the same bed configuration as the pool view units. All rooms are air-conditioned, come with a refrigerator, satellite television and a covered porch or balcony. Rates include tropical breakfast, use of the hotels kayaks, snorkeling equipment and beach loungers. Children under 18 are not permitted and the hotel accepts all major credit cards. The onsite restaurant and bar is open for three meals a day and specializes in Pacific Rim cuisine. Rumor has it; the breakfast menu features the freshest eggs on the island. The 24-hour reception desk can arrange a spa treatment, rental cars, tours and airport transfers

Avana Waterfront Apartments, Ph. (682) 20-836, Fax. (682) 21-530
PO Box 869, Rarotonga, Cook Islands
Website: www.avanacondos.co.ck
Email: avanco@oyster.net.ck

At the west end of the island, near the Ngatangiia passage, is where this ten-unit complex is located. The 4 newer deluxe self-contained studio units are air-conditioned and fully screened with refrigerator, microwave and dishwasher and have and come complete with a patio or deck.   The five two-bedroom self-contained townhouses are two-storied with ceiling fans, a large lounge and kitchen and bath downstairs with the two bedrooms and a second bath upstairs.   There is a large first floor patio downstairs and a smaller deck off of the master bedroom. The one three-bedroom self-contained townhouse is similar to the two bedroom units, with the addition of the third bedroom. The complex has a fresh water swimming pool, covered picnic area and barbecue for guests and the complex looks out at Muri Lagoon and across to an uninhabited island or *motu.*   There are plenty of lounge furniture on each deck as well as complimentary snorkeling equipment kayaks and dinghies to enjoy the lagoon.   Guests receive breakfast and fruit baskets upon arrival.   Rates for the studio units which feature a single king size bed are NZ$300.00, for single/double, with the two bedroom units, which contain a queen sized bed in the main bedroom and two single beds in the second bedroom renting for NZ$480.00. The two bedroom units will sleep up to five people utilizing the day bed in the lounge area.   The three-bedroom unit rents for NZ$535.00, with one king sized bed and two singles in the other two bedrooms and will sleep up to six comfortably. It is a short walk to the restaurants and shops in the Muri Beach area. Tours and rental vehicles can be arranged at the office.

Moderate

Lagoon Lodges, Ph. (682) 22-020, Fax (682) 22-021
P.O. Box 45, Rarotonga, <u>Cook Islands</u>
Website: <u>www.lagoonlodges.com</u>
E-mail: <u>lagoon@oyster.net.ck</u>

On the main road, near the Rarotongan Beach Resort, Lagoon Lodges offers 21 thatched-roof bungalows situated amongst a lovely garden, directly across from the west-facing beach. Original developer Des Eggleton helped build the airport back in 1973 fell in love with the island and a lovely young island girl by the name of Casey, and, as they say, the rest is history. I am sad to say The Eggleton's have recently sold the Lodges to a local group. Let's hope the new owner's continue with the care, cleanliness and pride established by the original owners. An example of that care is in the location of each bungalow within the setting, so as to offer privacy but yet encourage an intimacy of a village setting. It is no accident that they appear at the top of the moderate category, as Lagoon Lodges is one of my top picks for value in the moderate category. There are six studio units that sleep up to three people, the rate is NZ$245.00 for single/double. The six one bedroom bungalows that sleep up to four people go for NZ$280.00 for single/double. The seven two bedroom villas that sleep up to six persons, rent for NZ$315.00 for single/double. The two bedroom deluxe villas, with a bedroom and a bathroom on each of the two levels, rent for NZ$375.00 and sleep up to four people and are not suited for children. There is one three bedroom villa, with it's own private swimming pool, an extensive outdoor terrace and barbecue area. Two of the bedrooms have queen beds and the villa has a modern fully equipped kitchen with microwave, refrigerator/freezer and a large step down lounge complete with stereo/television and video. The three bedroom villa sleeps up to seven people and the rates are NZ$545.00 for single/double. All bungalows have an additional charge of NZ$65.00 per night for an additional adult (after the first two). In addition children 3-12 years old are an additional NZ$15.00 per night, children under three are free of charge. There is an on site terrace which serves breakfast in the mornings (additional cost) and airport transfers are available at NZ$20.00 per adult and NZ$10.00 for children. There is a large freshwater pool on site and snorkeling equipment is available at the office. Tours and rental bikes, scooters and cars can be arranged at the office.

The Lodge's also have a three bedroom, two-bath villa off site,  at Muri Beach that is available to rent. The villa features a fully equipped kitchen, with microwave oven, refrigerator/freezer and dishwasher. The open dining/lounge area has a T.V. video and stereo and opens onto an extensive covered terrace for outdoor dining on the wood deck. The freshwater pool comes with a gazebo and overlooks the white sand beach of the lagoon. Other amenities include a barbecue, kayak and snorkeling gear for your use during your visit at the villa. The bedrooms are all equipped with split king size beds. The villa is serviced three times a week and has a maximum occupancy of seven people. Rates for this villa are NZ$695 for single/double, with an additional NZ$65.00 for each adult beyond four and an additional NZ$15.00 for each child accompanying two adults

Palm Grove Resort, Ph. (682) 20-002, Fax (682) 21-998
P.O. Box 23, Rarotonga, <u>Cook Islands</u>
Website: <u>www.palmgrove.net</u>
E-mail: <u>beach@palmgrove.co.ck</u>

Down the road 3½ Km. South of Lagoon Lodges sits the Palm Grove, which is one of my top recommendations in this category. There are a total of 24 different bungalows and villas on this large resort like setting. Twelve of the bungalows are beach-front, six garden studios are laid out in a half circle around the BBQ area and the swimming pool, with four one bedroom superior units and one each of one, two and three bedroom bungalows placed with care amongst the grounds. All but the beachfront units are across the main road from the beach. The large fresh water swimming pool is located near their new restaurant and barbeque area for guests. In addition guests have use of snorkeling equipment and kayaks. Each unit is fully self-contained with private patios and decks at all units. Palm Grove is located near a supermarket and the round island bus stops at the front entrance. Laundry and babysitting services are available on site and rental vehicles and tours can be arranged at the desk. Rates are NZ$235.00 for single/twin/double for the six garden studios which have a king size and single bed. There are four one-bedroom superior garden units with air-conditioning, that rent for NZ$285.00 per night and they also have a king size and single bed. There is also a one-bedroom standard bungalow in the garden area that rents for NZ$235.00 per night. This unit has a king size bed and two single beds and the rate is NZ$235.00 per night single/twin/double. In all of the above units you can add a third adult for NZ$65.00 per night, and children under five are free of charge. There are also two villas in the garden area, one is a two bedroom bungalow and this rents for NZ$330.00 per night for up to four people. The bed configuration is two queen sized and two single beds, with a maximum of five people. The three-bedroom bungalow rents for the same amount, with the three-bedroom unit having a maximum of six people. Add an extra person to the villas for NZ$65.00 each. The eight beachfront studios which feature one king size bed or two singles rent for

NZ$3250.00 to NZ$360.00 for single double and have a maximum occupancy of two people. Children under five years of age are excluded from these units. All rates include complimentary tropical breakfast. Dinner is served nightly in the open air Yellow Hibiscus Restaurant, which is fast becoming a favorite island wide.

Aro'a Beachside Inn, Ph. (682) 22-166, Fax (682) 22-169
P.O. Box 2160, Rarotonga, <u>Cook Islands</u>
Website: <u>www.aroabeach.com</u>
E-mail: <u>aroa@cookislands.co.ck</u>

Jim Bruce is the proprietor of Aro'a Inn. You will recognize Jim as the guy with the straw hat, and this transplanted Hawaiian has moved his act from Lahaina, on Maui to Arorangi on Rarotonga. Look for his self installed kilo marker 21.1 as you drive past Arorangi, he is on the right hand side in front of an excellent swimming and snorkeling beach on the western, (sunset side) of Rarotonga. The units were designed to please the ladies, as Jim knows they are the ones that make decisions on where to stay. There are three units known as garden units, that unfortunately look out at the lagoon and not the garden, but maybe the garden will grow later, in the mean time enjoy the lagoon view, they rent for NZ$190.00/NZ$250.00/$300.00 for single/double/triple. The eight huge beachside deluxe studios rent for

NZ$320.00/NZ$350.00/NZ$400.00 for single/double/triple. Extra persons are NZ$50.00 per night with a maximum of three people in the garden studios and four people in the beachside units. All units are equipped with screens, ceiling fans and are fully self-contained. Snorkeling gear and kayaks are complimentary to guests. There is a covered deck on the edge of the lagoon known as the shipwreck hut, where one can relax and enjoy the sunset after a day of water sports. Two of the beachside units are handicapped accessible and each unit has a large covered wood deck with a table and chairs. In short all you need to enjoy a vacation in paradise. So fall asleep to the sound of the waves on the reef and be sure and tell Jim that Papa Mike sent you there. Saturday and Tuesday nights are Sunset Barbeque Nights with entertainment, call ahead to reserve your spot at the table.

Manea Beach Villas, Ph. (682) 25-336, Fax (682) 25-433
P.O. Box 440, Rarotonga, <u>Cook Islands</u>
Website: <u>www.maneabeachrarotonga.com</u>
E-mail: <u>stay@manea.co.ck</u>

This six-unit property is located on Muri Lagoon on the Eastern side of Rarotonga. It is close to the areas many restaurants and mini mart. The white clapboard units have spacious decks with outdoor furniture and overlook the lagoon. The four one-bedroom units have refrigerator, microwave, electric frying pan and coffee service. The air-conditioned bedroom has a queen-sized bed. The spacious lounge/dining area is equipped with T.V. and a large sliding door that faces the lagoon. There is one beachfront studio with lots of glass, you can lie in bed and view the lagoon, and so this doubles as the honeymoon suite, equipped with a large king-sized bed. The three-bedroom villa can sleep up to five people and is equipped with both air conditioning and fans. Basic room rates are listed as NZ$250.00 on an associated Website. The largest Villa, the vaulted ceiling three-bedroom, two bath, beachfront unit, sleeps up to five. Two bedrooms have king-sized beds and a third has a single bed. This unit is ideal for a large family or two couples and is a true home away from home, even including a carport. Adjacent to the villa is a huge outdoor deck and swimming pool with loads of outdoor furniture. This property was recently purchased by the Tepaki group, whose interests include Lagoon Lodges, Castaways, Manuia Beach Resort and the venerable Hilton/Sheraton hotel project that languishes on the west side, nearly twenty years since construction began.

Moana Sands Hotel & Villas, Ph. (682) 26-189, Fax (682) 22-189, P.O. Box 1007, Rarotonga, <u>Cook Islands</u>
Website: <u>www.moanasands.co.ck</u>
E-mail: <u>beach@moanasands.co.ck</u>

There are seventeen beach facing fully air-conditioned self-contained units in this three-story complex located in the village of Tititaveka on the south side of the island. Each has a great view of the lagoon and a patio to enjoy it on. Moana Sands has an excellent beach and swimming and snorkeling is directly in front of the hotel. Twelve of the units are studios and have a queen-sized bed as well as a single bed, refrigerator, and, while they don't come with a stove, they have toaster, coffee maker and electric frying pans. Kids are welcome and will enjoy the game room with T.V. and VCR. The third floor has five suites. In addition this facility has complimentary snorkeling equipment, kayaks, canoes and a barbeque area for guest use. There is an on-site Paw Paw Patch restaurant open daily for breakfast and dinner. Sundays they have a beach barbeque for guests and visitor alike. Rates are NZ$295.00 for the studios, single/double and an additional NZ$75.00 for a third person. Children are an additional NZ$45.00 in a studio. The third floor suites go for NZ$350.00, single/double/twin. No children or triples on the third floor are allowed.

Muri Beachcomber, Ph. (682) 21-022, Fax (682) 21-323
P.O. Box 379, Rarotonga, Cook Islands
Website: www.beachcomber.co.ck
E-Mail: muri@beachcomber.co.ck

Phil and Juliet Wells' Muri Beachcomber is in the heart of Muri Beach on the right just past Vara's Beach House. The 22-unit complex is spread around a large parcel with a fresh water creek flowing amongst the units. There are sixteen sea view units they rent for NZ$295.00 for a maximum of three people. The end sea view units #1, #10 and #14 are the most desirable being closest to the lagoon. These sea view units are restricted to adults only with no children under 12 allowed There are three garden units and these rent for NZ$255.00 for a maximum of five people. Kids are welcome in these units.

The upstairs garden unit is a two-bedroom unit and doubles as a family unit, the rates are NZ$300.00, with a maximum occupancy of six. In addition to the above, there are three water garden villas which feature microwaves air conditioning in bedroom, telephones a T.V. and VCR's, these rent for NZ$355.00 per day for up to five people. All units are self-contained, with well-equipped kitchens, ceiling fans, refrigerators, and ranges. All units are furnished with fresh fruit, milk and fruit juice on arrival. Muri Beachcomber is close to shops, restaurants and water sports. International transfers are included in room rates; tours and rental vehicles are available from the front desk. The round-island bus service, stops directly in front of Muri Beachcomber, providing convenient access to the whole island.

Club Raro, Ph. (682) 22-415, Fax (682) 24-415
P.O. Box 483, Rarotonga, Cook Islands
Website: www.clubraro.co.ck
E-mail: holiday@clubraro.co.ck

Just 2 km. east of Avarua, on the beach side of the main road, lays the 55-unit Club Raro. The activity oriented medium-sized resort has an in house restaurant serving all three meals. There is a bar in the restaurant area as well as one by the fresh water pool. The individual rooms surround the grounds and the pool, which is located near the beach. There are 20 garden units, each with a queen-sized bed and one single bed. The 20-poolside rooms share the same room configuration, while the 15 new beachfront units have a queen-sized bed and each room is equipped with a T.V. Club Raro is actually much more attractive once you enter the large lobby than it appears from the street. Also located within the lobby are a T.V. and VCR as well as a desk for Internet and Email access. Rates are NZ$140 00 for studio units single/twin/double while garden units are NZ$160.00 single/twin/double, from there the poolside units are renting for NZ$170.00 single/double. Beachfront units were renting for NZ$210.00 and all of these rates were based on "Internet Special Pricing," with a minimum of five nights. Extra adults are NZ$60 and children 12 and under are free when sharing with adults. Late check out is available for 50% of the room rate. Each of the clean, tidy, tiled units has air-conditioning, coffee service and a refrigerator.

Little Polynesian, Ph. (682) 24-280, Fax (682) 21-585
P.O. Box 366, Rarotonga, <u>Cook Islands</u>
Website: littlepolynesian.com
E-mail: <u>littlepoly@beach.co.ck</u>

This secluded beachside complex has attained resort status with the addition of their new intimate restaurant. Located on the main road in Titikaveka, just down from the Moana Sands. There are eight beachfront studios and one cottage in this romantic retreat. Nestled amongst a grove of coconut palms are a barbecue area, tables and hammocks a few steps from the lagoon. There are kayaks and snorkeling gear available. Children under 12 are excluded from Little Polynesian.

Weddings and honeymoons are their specialty at Little Polynesian and their cottage unit is an excellent honeymoon suite, just steps from the lagoon. The Little Polynesian is located on an excellent swimming and snorkeling beach, where occasionally giant manta rays happen by the reef. The locally crafted bungalows and cottage are all fully self-contained, with a king sized bed or two single beds, refrigerator and ceiling fans. Rates are NZ$250.00 per night for single/double/twin in the beachfront units, add NZ$75.00 for a third  adult. The beautiful lagoon-side cottage rents for NZ$290.00 per night for one or two persons.

Sunset Resort Rarotonga, Ph. (682) 28-028, Fax (682) 28-026
P.O. Box 483, Rarotonga, Cook Islands
Website: www.thesunsetresort.com
E-mail: welcome@sunsetresort.com

There is a mix of 35 self-contained studios, two one-bedroom suites and one two-bedroom suite in Sunset Resorts complex about 5 Km. West of Avarua. The complex is in a section known as Black Rock and is just prior to reaching the Edgewater complex on the main road. Look for the sign on your right. Each unit has a deck to enjoy the nightly sunset; eight of the studio units are beachfront with the other units located around the pool and adjacent gardens. All units contain king-sized beds and a single bed and all are air-conditioned. There is a large pool and adjacent bar that is open every evening. Sunday features a sunset barbecue around the pool and there are seven restaurants within walking distance of the property. The lagoon is directly below the units and snorkeling and kayaks are offered complimentary to guests. The quick-witted manager and his friendly staff can arrange scooter or car rentals, sightseeing and outer island excursions. Rates start at NZ$206 per room single or double for garden units, NZ$266 per room single or double for beachfront studio and add another $27.00 for a supreme beachfront studio. The two bedroom unit goes for NZ$439 for up to a maximum of four people. Add a third person in a beachside unit and it's another NZ$30, and they'll pick you up and drop you at the airport for another NZ$20. All prices include island breakfast of cereal, toast, coffee and fruit. This property, in a smaller version, was previously known as the Rarotongan Sunset.

Puaikura Reef Lodges, Ph. (682) 23-537, Fax (682) 21-537
P.O. Box 397, Rarotonga, <u>Cook Islands</u>
Website: <u>www.puaikura.co.ck</u>
E-mail: <u>accommodations@puaikura.co.ck</u>

Owner Barry Warner's Puaikura Reef Lodges are across the road from the beach on the southwest part of the island, ten km. from Avarua. The lodges are a great option for a family; each of the 12 one-bedroom, self-contained units has a separate bedroom as well as having two single beds in the large living/dining area of the unit. The studios have a divider that separates the sleeping area from the living area and feature the same two twin bed combination. There is a small swimming pool, honesty bar as well as a covered barbeque area for the guests. Book ahead as this property is popular and often booked far in advance, with many guests returning year after year. Rates are NZ$165.00 for single/double in standard one bedroom and superior studio units. A third adult is an additional NZ40.00 and for each child aged 2-15 adds $15.00, with children under two free of charge. In recent years Puakura Lodges has added an adjacent three bedroom bungalow that rent for NZ$220.00 for double, NZ$300 for four people and NZ$380.00 for six people.

Castaway Beach Villas, Ph. (682) 21-546, Fax (682) 25-546
P.O. Box 693, Rarotonga, <u>Cook Islands</u>
Website: <u>www.castawayvillas.com</u>
E-Mail: <u>relax@castawaysvillas.com</u>

This popular property, for years was known as Ati's after former owner Ati Robertson, is on the beach south of the village of Arorongi. A Longtime history of owner/operators have created a quiet intimate lodging with reasonable prices.. There are twelve bungalows on the property, four of which are beachfront units. The flags of all nations represented by guests fly on their flagpoles. Guests from small African nations may want to bring their own flag. Previous owners worked hard upgrading the property and completing two new fully air-conditioned superior villas, next to the pool, these rent for NZ$200.00 for single/double. The four beachfront units are cooled by ceiling fans and these also rent for NZ$200.00 for single/double, add NZ$40.00 for an extra person. The other four units are known as standard garden and rent for NZ$130 for single/double with an additional NZ$40.00 for a third person. Children aged 5-14 sharing a room with parents are charged NZ$25.00 for the first child and NZ$15.00 for the second child. Airport pick up is free in their minibus, airport return is NZ15.00 for adults and NZ$7.50 for children. Castaways was recently acquired by the Tepaki group, which holdings include Manuia Beach Resort, Lagoon Lodges and other lodgings, no changes are planned for the property.

The on site Crusoe's restaurant has long been a favorite on the island and Sunday night is Feast night at Crusoe's, with a barbecue on their white sand beach for NZ$20.00. Dinners are served at Crusoe's six nights a week; they take outsiders, but call ahead for reservations. The restaurant is closed on Mondays. Wednesday Night sunset barbeques are well attended, call ahead for reservations. Complimentary breakfast is served daily to residents.

Aroko Bungalows, Ph. (682) 23-625, Fax (682) 24-625
P.O. Box 850, Rarotonga, Cook Islands
Website: www.arokobungalows.com
E-mail: aroko@bungalows.co.ck

These bungalows face Muri Lagoon past Pacific Divers and Sokala Villas; they are the last accommodation on Muri Lagoon, prior to reaching Avana Passage. Of the eleven units, six are lagoon view and five are garden view. The bungalows are all studios, with a small gas range, refrigerator, radio and basic cooking and dining equipment as well as a table and chair for two. Each bungalow has it's own small patio that overlooks the garden, with partial views of the lagoon, or the lagoon front units which have full lagoon views. Cooling is via ceiling fans and each unit has a full bath with shower. Lagoon view bungalows, especially the ones at the front of the property are in constant demand and you will need to book well in advance to reserve these units. There is a cozy feel about the place, clean grounds with a laundry room that guests can use for NZ$2.00 wash and NZ$3.00 to dry. The lagoon in front has coral so you need your reef walkers to get to the sand beach, which is about 40 yards away. The location is good, close to a market and within walking distance of several restaurants. Tours and rentals can be arranged at the desk and there are plenty of shops, restaurants and water sports activities within walking distance of the bungalows. Rates for the five garden view bungalows are NZ$130.00 for single/double while the lagoon front bungalows rent for NZ$150.00 per night. There is a minimum stay requirement of two days and they offer a 10% discount on continuous stays of seven nights or longer. With flight arrival and departures coming at unlikely times, you may be charged for early arrival and or late departure costs, it is best to discuss this with management at the time you make your reservations, so that you understand the costs and have no surprises on your bill. Airport transfers are NZ$10.00 each way, per person. These rates represent a bargain to most other self-contained bungalows in the Muri Beach area, but keep in mind they are fairly small and linens are changed every four days, In addition there are no T.V. or phones in the bungalows, but if you can live without some of these amenities, Aroko bungalows offer a good value.

Manuia Beach Resort, Ph. (682) 22-461, Fax (682) 22-464
P.O. Box 700, Rarotonga, Cook Islands
Website: www.manuia.co.ck
E-mail: rooms@manuia.co.ck

Twenty-four thatched bungalows are situated on a west facing sandy beach in Arorangi Village, just 7½ km. west of Avarua, past the Crown Beach Resort. The resort is a, "kid free zone" with no children under 12 allowed. The ten beachfront bungalows are equipped with a king-sized bed, refrigerator, coffee service, air conditioning and ceiling fans. The fourteen garden units are equipped with a queen-sized bed in lieu of the king. Each unit has a covered deck with a table and chairs. Snorkeling equipment, beach towels and tropical breakfast is complimentary to guests. Manuia Beach has an in-house restaurant and bar right on the beach near their large swimming pool. This boutique hotel has all the services of a much larger complex, while retaining the charm of a small inn. Their location is on a good snorkeling and swimming beach, close to the many restaurants in the area and only five minutes from the golf course and airport. Rates are NZ$480.00 for the garden units single/double and NZ$650.00 for the beachfront units. Add a third adult for NZ$110.00. Manuia Beach's location is excellent and if you are looking for a restful spot with all services on site Manuia is a good choice. If you want to venture out, here are plenty of good restaurants within walking distance of the resort so you can eat on site or if you prefer visit the areas varied selection of restaurants. The island bus stops at the front entry to the property. The Manuia Beach Resort was recently purchased by the Tepaki group, which plans no major change in the hotel property.

Muri Beach Resort, Ph. (682) 22-779, Fax. (682) 22-775
PO Box 146, Rarotonga, Cook Islands
Website: www.muribeachresort.com
Email: relax@muribeachresort.com

These fully furnished deluxe units are located on the beach in the corner of Muri Lagoon. There were originally two units, but an additional four units were completed in years past and then three more garden units were completed about four years ago. All units are separate, fully air conditioned, with double sized Jacuzzi tubs in each unit. There are private phones, T.V. and VCR's in each unit. The freshwater pool is the largest outside of the major resorts and Muri Beach Resort offers free use of snorkeling and kayaks. Some of the finest snorkeling on the island is right in front of Muri Beach Resort. Children under 18 years of age are not permitted. Rates are NZ$225 per night, single and double on the garden unit, and NZ$300.00 single/double for the five lagoon view units. Early bird special rates are NZ$165.00 for garden view and NZ$195.00 for the lagoon view units, visit the Website for conditions of early bird special rates. This hotel was previously known as Shangri La, Under new ownership, the owners unit has been split up into two units and the total units is now in the neighborhood of fourteen.

Rarotonga Beach Bungalows, Ph. (682) 27-030, Fax (682) 27-031
P.O. Box 3045, Rarotonga, Cook Islands
Website: www.rarobeachbungalows.com
E-mail: swim@rarobeachbungalows.co, ck

One of the islands newest places to stay, the 5 pleasant and spacious (700 sq.ft) bungalows are nestled in a mini-village on the south side of the island on the main road near the Moana Sands Hotel. The units face the lagoon within a marine protected wildlife area and therefore the surrounding waters are teaming with fish. Use of snorkeling equipment, kayaks, lounge chairs and a paperback library are all complimentary to guests. The theme of all the villas is old world Polynesian and the furniture and decorations in the bungalows are quite authentic. The exteriors are natural wood, raised floors on stilts and natural woven palm frond roofs complete the native charm of the complex. Rates are NZ$545.00 for lagoon view units and NZ$595.00 for beach front units. You can add a third person to your bungalow for an additional NZ$50.00. Each unit is fully self-contained with a kitchenette, fans, toaster, cd player and a microwave, which while not part of the "old island charm", is a welcome convenience. The other welcome "new world" convenience is the air conditioner next to the king-sized bed. The island bus runs directly in front of Rarotonga Beach Bungalows and there is a convenience store and restaurant within walking distance. Children under 12 are not permitted. Rates for long term (more than 7 days) are negotiable. A great option for that maximum rest, get away from it all vacation, sell some of that Google stock and come snorkel a month away.

Sunhaven Beach Bungalows, Ph. (682) 28-465 Fax. (682) 28464
PO Box 100, Rarotonga, Cook Islands
Website: www.ck/sunhaven
E-Mail: sunhaven@beachbungalows.co.ck

Owners Dennis and Patti Hogan have established a coconut tree lined beachhead on the sunset (west) side of Rarotonga just south of Arorangi. Eight of the nine tasteful bungalows and studios are clustered around the freshwater pool that sits directly in front of the lagoon on a quiet secluded location. Kayaks, snorkeling gear and hammocks await the guests on arrival, their small on site café is well stocked for breakfast, lunch and afternoon snacks around the pool. Rates are NZ$270.00 for a beachfront bungalow, with similar pricing on adjacent bungalows and studios. The single garden bungalow is slightly less at NZ$230, with the smaller standard studio available for NZ$195.00. The Studio Suite and Deluxe Studio are the only air-conditioned units available, but with the prevailing coastal breezes and ample fans, your stay promises to be comfortable and restful. Sunhaven has its own Private Van and airport transfers in comfort are available for NZ$17.50 per person return.

Sunrise Beach Bungalows, Ph./Fax. (682) 20-417
PO Box 251, Rarotonga, Cook Islands
Website: www.sunrise.co.ck
Email: motel@sunrise.co.ck

Caryn Chilwell's 8 bungalows are just 2 Km. from Muri Lagoon, on the main road in the village of Ngatangiia. Each bungalow is designed for independent living, with refrigerator, kitchenette and sunny covered patios. While not directly on the water, the ocean is only twenty meters away. The cool individual bungalows each have a queen and single bed or can be adapted to three singles. On site there is a swimming pool, gas barbeque and guest laundry. Snorkeling equipment is complimentary to guests. Rates at the time this is written are a very reasonable NZ$110.00 per unit for beachfront, up to three people. Garden units are NZ$100.00 for the same three people max. These are some of the lowest rates for air=conditioned units on the island.

Reefcomber Sunset Beach Motel, Ph. (682) 25-673, Fax.
(682) 25-672 P.O. Box 373, Rarotonga, Cook Islands

Website: www.soltel.co.ck
E-mail: solomon@oyster.net.ck

Located in the black rock area, the Reefcomber has 4 self-contained bungalows, four garden studios, three beach and ocean view studios and a self-contained one-bedroom studio with family room. Each bungalow/studio is air-conditioned with a queen size and single bed, ceiling fan, shower and bath, breakfast bar and refrigerator. The units are close to restaurants shops and the golf course. Rental bikes, scooters cars and various tours can be arranged at the office. Combined vacations with their Aitutaki property Maina Sunset can also be arranged. The Reefcomber is on white sand, west-facing beach, with excellent snorkeling in the adjacent lagoon. Lots of restaurants are in the area as well as the golf course and shops. The around island bus stops at the end of the entry lane, which is only forty yards from the motel. Rates are NZ$200.00 for the beachfront units and NZ$175.00 for the garden view or ocean view units, one of which is a one bedroom unit suitable for families.

Shell & Crafts Cottages, Ph. (682) 22-275, Fax. (682) 22-270
PO Box 245, Rarotonga, Cook Islands
Website: www.shellbungalows.co.ck
E-Mail: Murishells@hotmail.com

This small three-unit complex is directly adjacent to the Pacific Resort, while not lagoon front the units are a quiet stroll from the lagoon. Close to a variety of shops and restaurants in the Muri Lagoon neighborhood. These, open-plan modern fully self-contained bungalows are screened and come equipped with ceiling fans and feature attached decks. Depending on seasons, rates are between NZ$85.00 to NZ$100,00 Book direct by E-Mail to the owner.

The Cooks Oasis, Ph. (682) 28-213, Cell. (682) 70-366
PO Box 497, Rarotonga, Cook Islands
Website: www.cookislandsoasis.com
Email: info@thecooks.co.ck

The former Oasis Village Motel has been converted to seven island flavored studio units for 1-4 people. Owners Joan and Jeff Cook promise to make your trip to Rarotonga a memorable experience for all the good reasons. Their Black Rock location is close to a variety of restaurants and shops and only a short walk from the beach. Complimentary use of snorkeling equipment, reef shoes and you are welcome to throw some shrimp on the communal barbeque. All studios are fully self-contained with either a king-size or twin beds. The on-site cool off pool is centrally located to all units. Rates are NZ$170.00 for single/double and triples are NZ$200:00. If you stay three days or more your breakfast is provided on the first morning of your stay, compliments of the owners. Discounts for long stays of six days or more. Need air-conditioning? It is available for an additional NZ$20:00 per night. Airport transfers are available for NZ$40.00 return for adults and children over 10, 5 to 9 year olds are NZ$20.00 and the little ones go for free.

Kura's Kabana's, Ph. (682) 27-010, Fax. (682) 27-025
PO Box 904, Rarotonga, Cook Islands
Website: www.kkabanas.co.ck
Email: kkabanas@oyster.net.ck

There are four one bedroom beachfront cabanas, suitable for up to two people, three family beach view studios for a family of four and a separate hideaway cottage a couple hundred yards away on the inland road. The cabanas and studios are directly adjacent to the beach on the far end of Muri lagoon, near the Muri Beach Resort. The hideaway cottage is a short walk from the beach. Rates for the beachfront cabanas as well as the family studios are

NZ$200.00 per night. The hideaway cottage rents for NZ$120.00 per night. Discounts for extended stays.

Daydreamer Apartments, Ph. (682) 25-965, Fax. (682) 78-083
PO Box 1048, Rarotonga, Cook Islands
Website: www.daydreamer.co.ck
Email: daydream@daydreamer.co.ck

Five spacious apartments in a secluded garden on the Southern sunset side of Rarotonga await couples, family and groups. The apartments feature high ceilings, separate bedrooms, ceiling fans and fully equipped kitchens. The living area of each apartment opens onto private verandahs and a white sand beach is only a short walk away across the road. One-bedroom apartments, feature a queen sized bed as well as a day bed in the living area. Rates for the spacious one bedroom units are NZ$140.00 for single/double/triple, while the two bedroom apartments, with a queen sized bed in the master bedroom and two twin bed in the second bedroom, rent for NZ$195.00. The two-bedroom units can sleep up to five people with an extra bed placed in the living area.

Tiana's Beach Bungalows, Ph. (672) 26-00 Fiji, Cook Islands
Website: www.tianas.com
Email: info@tianas.com

Located beachfront on popular Muri lagoon these four one-bedroom and two studio bungalows offer very good value. All units are roomy and fully self-contained. The two studios are right on the beach, with the four one bedroom units are screened from the beach by ironwood and palm trees, but less than 10 yards from the beach. The units are within walking distance of a variety of restaurants, an Internet café and convenience store. Rates are NZ$120.00 for two people in a studio units, while the one-bedroom bungalows rent for NZ$150.00. Units are serviced Monday to Friday and prices include use of the communal kayak. Airport transfers are available for NZ$15.00 per person (one way) Early check in and late check out is negotiable.

Budget

Paradise Inn, Ph. (682) 20-544, Fax (682) 22-544
P.O. Box 223, Rarotonga, <u>Cook Islands</u>
Website: <u>www.paradiseinnrarotonga.com</u>
E-mail: <u>paradise@oyster.net.ck</u>

Paradise Inn is a great bet if you are looking to be close to shopping and Rarotonga's principal city of Avarua. This property was once the largest dance hall in the South Pacific, prior to its reincarnation as a sixteen unit Inn. The Paradise Inn has fourteen units on two open walkways and is situated within walking distance of a wide variety of restaurants, nightclubs and

cultural activities. The hotel has a spacious lounge and terrace overlooking the sea. The communal honor bar insures plenty of liquid refreshment and the deck is a popular meeting point for guests. The entire staff is friendly and helpful and insures that your stay is enjoyable. The standard units are split-level with a double bed in the loft and single or day bed in the lower portion. All units are self-contained, bright and airy, the cost for each standard room is NZ$89.00/NZ$111.00/NZ$121.00 for single/double/triple. Two of the units are on the second floor and can be combined to form a family unit that can sleep up to six and rents for NZ$142 per night. In addition to the fourteen standard units, Paradise has two budget single units that rent for NZ$66 per night. To my thinking, Paradise Inn provides some of the best value in lodging that Rarotonga has to offer. Watch out for their killer cats, Trouble and Trouble, as they will likely prowl through your room in search of handouts. This property is the perfect blend for the business traveler, being within walking distance of Avarua, yet offering a great deck to relax on after a day of battling commerce. The children under 12 rule is not strictly enforced, so if you have a child or two close to 12, they still may able to accommodate you. Crying babies are not to be encouraged, but the Roosters start up about 3:00 AM island wide, so small distractions are to be expected.

Tiare Village, Ph. (682) 23-466, Fax (682) 21-874
P.O. Box 719. Rarotonga, <u>Cook Islands</u>
Website: <u>www.tiarevillage.co.ck</u>
E-mail: <u>kiaorana@tiarevillage.co.ck</u>

For those on a very limited budget, Tiare Village may be just the ticket. It is located 2 Km. West of Avarua off the *Ara Matua* on Kaikaveka and is at the far end of the airport, within walking distance of the stores, restaurants and bars in Avarua. There are a variety of rooms available in the main house and on the grounds. The main house has a triple that rents for NZ$60. There are three self-contained chalets that run NZ$25/NZ$44 single/double. In addition clustered around the pool are six self-contained poolside double units that cost NZ$70 per day. Tiare Village is a popular budget spot for divers and the friendly staff can help arrange dive trips or other excursions. There is a T.V. in the guest lounge at the main house as well as a pleasant verandah for those rainy days. Since Tiare Village is a distance from the beach, you will want to make sure you bring along protection from those pesky mosquitoes. The grounds are home to a variety of fruit trees and guests are welcome to pick fresh from the trees. Expect to meet a host of young backpackers from Europe, New Zealand and Australia at the Tiare, for the location has been passed along by word of mouth long before E-mail and Websites were around. Tiare Village will meet you at the airport when you arrive in Rarotonga from your International flight. Transfers when you leave are extremely reasonable at only NZ$6.50. Tiare Village is also very reasonable for those of us arriving on Air New Zealand from Los Angeles. Early check in is a quite reasonable NZ$15.00 per room, which will seem wonderful at 5:30 AM after a twelve-hour plane flight. Tiare has suffered from some negative trip reports on the Internet, but when I visited the place was about what is to be expected of a budget lodging, clean and usable. Cash is king at Tiare, no credit cards accepted, discounts for extended stays. When I revisited Tiare Village in 2008 to update the listing for the second edition, I was amazed that the prices were still the same as back in 2003, Tiare was a bargain back then and obviously remains an excellent value.

Maiana Guesthouse, Ph. (682) 20-438,
Fax (682) 20-436 Rarotonga, <u>Cook Islands</u>
Website: <u>www.maianaguesthouse.co.ck</u>
E-mail: <u>maiana@oyster.net.ck</u>

This is a fairly new budget accommodation on Rarotonga, situated on the south side of the island across the main road from Turoa beach, just past Wigmore's market. Ina and Mano welcome backpackers and budget travelers to their guesthouse. There is a barbeque area for cooking as well as a community kitchen for guests. Feel free to use the laundry and the clothesline. Next door to Maiana is a bakery and small restaurant for breakfast and lunch and the island bus goes by the property. Excursions and car rental are available and Mano offers free airport pick up to guests. Rates are NZ$18 in the "dormitory" room. The eight single/double/triple accommodations rent for a reasonable rate of NZ$40/NZ$45/NZ$55. The location is a fifteen-minute walk from

Muri Beach, which has numerous restaurants for meals. One feature I found appealing was that each room had a lockable cupboard in the communal kitchen and there were two separate cooking areas. Although bathrooms are shared, there are six bath/shower rooms for the nine units, which should eliminate overcrowding. There is a beach directly across the street with good snorkeling and Maina will furnish complementary snorkeling equipment and kayaks to guests. I sent a couple from Montana to Ina & Mano and they loved the month they spent there, watching the husband and wife team run the place, was better than a snowstorm in Gardiner, Montana.

Aremango Guesthouse, Ph. (682) 24-362, Fax (682) 24-363
P.O. Box 3115, Rarotonga, <u>Cook Islands</u>
Website: <u>www.ck/aremango/</u>
E-mail: <u>aremango@oyster.net.ck</u>

Located in the heart of Muri Beach on the right just past Muri Beach Resort, this guesthouse has 10 bedrooms and 34 beds to accommodate a variety of different combinations of lodging. There is a fully equipped kitchen and three bathrooms to share, host Edwin Taio offers to pick you up free at the airport if you stay at the guesthouse. There is a covered exterior lounge area with books and games and swimming and snorkeling is only a short walk away. All rooms are screened and come equipped with fans. Water sports, shops and restaurants are all within walking distance from this clean and comfortable guesthouse. Rates are NZ$18.00 for a dormitory room. For private rooms with shared baths rates are twin/double/triple NZ$40.00/NZ$40.00/NZ$54.00

Kii Kii Motel, Ph. (682) 21-937, Fax (682) 22-937
P.O. Box 68, Rarotonga, <u>Cook Islands</u>
Website: <u>www.kikimotel.co.ck</u>
E-mail: <u>relax@kikimotel.co.ck</u>

Harry and Pauline Napa's Kii Kii Motel has evolved over a period of nearly forty years. Starting with four units in the sixties the motel has evolved into the current configuration of 24 budget, standard and deluxe units in a traditional motel configuration that looks like it would be more at home in New Mexico along old Route 66 than gracing a point on Rarotonga. Besides the 24 units on the northwestern side of the island, Kii Kii rents, by the week, 6 fully furnished two-bedroom cottages on the west side of the island. The units are all self-contained (full kitchens), clean and very pleasant. There is a swimming pool overlooking the ocean and guests have access to a barbeque area. Kii Kii is on the main road less than 3 kilometers from Avarua. Rates for budget units are, NZ$70/NZ$90 for single/double. The newer standard and substantially larger west wing units rent for a very reasonable NZ$95/NZ$120/NZ$155/NZ$185 for single/double/triple/quad. The deluxe beachside units run NZ$120/130 single and NZ$150/160 double. The two-bedroom holiday beach cottages rent for NZ$435 per week. Airport transfers are NZ$9.00 each way.

Rarotonga Backpackers, Ph. (682) 21-590
P.O. Box 3103, Rarotonga, <u>Cook Islands</u>
Website: <u>www.rarotongabackpackers.com</u>
E-mail: <u>stay@rarotongabackpackers.com</u>

Since my original visit in 2003 Rarotonga Backpackers has undergone amazing expansion. The original hillside location just inland from Arorangi is going strong, but owners Paul and Rebecca have been up to far more than cleaning the pool and clearing weeds with that weed whacker.

Location #3 the latest addition to Rarotonga Backpackers is situated just off the main road in Avarua, directly behind Foodland, in what was formerly May's Guesthouse, it is known as **Townside**. It seems that May's and Rarotonga Backpackers are involved in some joint marketing of this property. Besides this listing, you will find a listing under Townhouse Backpackers, In any case, this converted five-bedroom home offers a variety of single/double/triple and quad rooms within the converted house, as well as a dormitory room for the really budget conscious. Shared kitchen and bath facilities are available. You will find plenty of shops, bars and restaurants a short walk away in the main town. Rates for the dormitory bunk beds start at NZ$20.00, rates for bedrooms are NZ$40.00/$48.00/$66.00/$80.00 for single, double, triple or quad.

Location #2 is known as **Beachside**, which is a larger complex on the beach in Arorongi, just past the Edgewater Resort and Dive Raro. Scattered among the complex are beachfront studios, suites, a beach house and hut as well as a variety of dormitory rooms. Facilities include a pool, barbeque, shared kitchen facilities and one thing that will brighten the day of any backpacker, plenty of hot water showers. Internet access is available on site, with plenty of shops, stores restaurants and bars within walking distance. Rates in the dormitory rooms start at a reasonable NZ$20.00 per day. Individual bedrooms go for NZ$40.00/$48.00/$66.00 for single/double/triple. Rooms with baths go for NZ$66/$75 for double/triple. Beachfront fully contained Studios are NZ$125.00 for single/double and NZ$135.00/$150.00 for 3 or 4 people. There is also beach huts available for NZ$80.00 for single double as well as a full on beach house for NZ$100.00 for single/double and NZ$120.00 for 3 or 4 people. Not yet listed on their website is a home behind the beachouse and about 25 meters from the beach, known as Beach Bach, rates for this unit are NZ$90.00 for single/double and NZ$100 for triple. As you can see there is pretty much something for everyone at the Beachside.

Location #1, the original location, now known as **Hillside** is still going strong. Amenities include a swimming pool, fully equipped communal kitchen, laundry, Internet, phone/fax service and free airport transfers. Owners Paul and Rebecca will rent you a scooter, bicycle, snorkel gear and even a surfboard at this budget facility. The very reasonable rates are dormitory rooms NZ$16.00 per night, single/double are NZ$35.00/NZ$42.00, with poolside units listed at NZ$69.00 per night for single/double and NZ$81.00 for triple. For long stays or group rates contact the owners. Where is my old backpack anyway?

Vara's Beach House, Ph. (682) 23-156, Fax (682) 22-619
P.O. Box 434, Rarotonga, Cook Islands
Website: www.varas.co.ck
E-mail backpack@varasbeach.co.ck

Long a fixture with younger travelers and backpackers, Vara's offers some of the least expensive accommodations in the Muri Beach area. The units are scattered over Vara Hunter's property and offer a variety of sleeping arrangements. Self contained beach studios rent for NZ$90.00, single NZ$120.00, double and NZ$150.00 for triple and families up to four. They have an ensuite bathroom and kitchen. The dormitory units, with shared kitchen and bathroom are NZ$25.00 per person. A double or twin room is $48.00 per night, with a shared kitchen and bath. A double with ensuite bath and a shared kitchen is NZ$75.00 per night. A self-contained apartment with private bath and kitchen is NZ$135.00. Varas will pick you up at the airport free of charge, as long as you are on an international flight. When you leave they will take you back to the airport for NZ$10.00. The beach units are popular with younger visitors and at times can be quite loud, I prefer the villa units at the top of the hill, the view is spectacular and the breezes keep the units' comfortable day or night. The villa has three bedrooms that share a kitchen and bathroom and depending on your fellow guests are far quieter than the units near the beach. The staff at Vera's is extremely friendly and go out of their way to help the guests. Rates may vary somewhat from what is shown above, the variety of combinations make it nearly impossible to list them all. The staff will be happy to explain your options once you explain your requirements. Rates quoted are for a minimum of three nights, costs slightly higher for short stays.

Ariana Bungalows, Ph. (682) 21-546, Fax (682) 25-546 P.O. Box 693, Rarotonga, <u>Cook Islands</u> E-Mail: <u>relax@ariana.co.ck</u>

The new owners at Ariana Bungalows, Eve Arietitototikai and Suse MacGillivray, are a couple of Kiwi-Cook Islanders with Irish and Scotch ancestry and they have been busy updating the 2 acre site 3 kilometers north of Avarua just off the main road. Turn right at the Big Brown Mart and head inland about 150 meters; it's on your left. Ariana has been an island mainstay for the budget crowd for many years and these two busy ladies plan on bringing the place into the new millennium. While work continues on the three additional bungalows, dorm rooms and hostel units the rates on the five fully renovated bungalows are NZ$70.00/$80.00 for a single/double, with triples at NZ$100.00. The dorm and hostel units, which should be complete by the end of the year, will rent for NZ$25.00 per person in the dorm, and NZ$30.00/$35.00 per person (or NZ$60.00-$70.00 per room) for the hostel. Call ahead to arrange airport transfers at NZ$30.00 roundtrip. Ariana is a ten-minute walk from the nearest beach, a short bus ride away from Muri Beach or Avarua. The site is home to a variety of fruit, which are free to residents as is the fresh water pool, TV room and adjacent library. If you get on Eve's good side, I am told she will offer you a specially made latte or cappuccino, from her espresso machine tucked away in the back of her mobile office. Situated amongst fruit trees, coconut palms and flowering bushes, Ariana offers the traveler a great spot to recharge the batteries, lying next to the pool waiting for the mangoes to ripen.

Are Renga Motel, Ph. (682) 20-050, Fax (682) 29-223
P.O. Box 223, Rarotonga, <u>Cook Islands</u>
Website: <u>www.arerenga.com</u>
E-mail: <u>arerenga@oyster.net.ck</u>

This 20-unit complex is spread amongst an egg farm on the main road in popular Arorangi, on the left hand side of the main road just past the Manuia Beach Hotel. While they charge a nominal price for eggs, cheapest price on the island, according to management, fruit in season is free to guests at the office. The reasonable prices start at NZ$40.00/NZ$60.00 for a single/double and while the units vary in size and location; all have attached toilets and showers. Shared twins are NZ$20.00 per person, not quite sure how that differs from a double, which is NZ$60.00. Cooking facilities, and a paperback library are in separate areas. Rates are negotiable for long-term stays and if you pay in advance you can figure to pay about NZ$300 a week for a double. Management is friendly and accommodating, just don't expect to be on the beach for these rates. The beach is across the street about fifty meters and the around island public bus stops at the entrance to the complex. They will pick you up at the airport for free, but charge you NZ$5.00 for the return transfer

Atupa Orchid Units, Ph. (682) 28-543, Fax (682) 28-546
P.O. Box 64, Rarotonga, <u>Cook Islands</u>
E-mail: <u>Ingrid@atupaorchid.co.ck</u>

Atupa Orchid Units are in Avarua on a back road that parallels the airport. While somewhat remote this budget accommodation is quiet, clean and friendly with an owner Ingrid Caffery that matches the feel of her property. There are two two-bedroom units that rent for NZ$80.00 per day. She has a one-bedroom cottage that rents for $70.00 per day, single/double. She also has a studio with a large verandah that rents for NZ$60.00 a day. The 'blue house' is a shared residence with three bedrooms, two of which have two single beds and one of which has a double and single bed. Rooms in the blue house are NZ$35.00 for single or NZ$22.00 per bed for shared bedroom. Kitchen and baths are shared and there is a nice covered patio at the front of the unit. All units at Atupa Orchid are self-contained, with full bathrooms. The owner places flowers and fruits in the units for your arrival and airport transfers are only NZ$5.00 per person. You are welcome to share the fruit on site when ripe. Ingrid, a German transplant conducts island tours for German speaking visitors.

Mount View Lodges, Ph. (682) 29-491
PO Box 862, Rarotonga, <u>Cook Islands</u>
Website: <u>www.mountviewlodges.co.ck</u>
Email: <u>greatstay@mountviewlodges.co.ck</u>

Shona Pitt, proprietor of Mount View Lodges will warn you about the idiosyncrasies of her six cottages, she will tell you about Michael Scooby John, her short legged island dog and head of security. She will explain about Bonnie, the neighbor's cat, who will beg for food at your cottage. She will explain her office hours as, "when I am home and the light is on." She may even warn you about her grandchildren who visit on occasion. If she sounds scary, her website warns, not to be scared of her, "that's just the way she looks." The website also states that she is open to bribery and is partial to chocolates and good wine. I don't know about you, but it sounds like my kind of place.

All six cottages are open plan studios, except Unit #2, which is a family unit with a double bedroom, a single bedroom and a open plan main room that can be partitioned off with bunks and a single bed. Rates on unit #2 are negotiable, depending on the number of people in your party and how much wine and chocolate you brought with you. All cottages are free standing and all but Unit #6 has patios or verandahs, overlooking the neighboring mountains. Rates on all units start at

NZ$35.00/$45.00 for single/double, which is negotiable depending on length of stay, who referred you, quality of bribes and the mood of management. Management states that rates may change according to demand and reserves the right to refuse bookings. For those brave enough to stay at Mount View, it is a short walk across the road to the beach and the bus stop.

Aquarius Rarotonga (Ph. (682) 21-003, Fax (682) 21-005
Near Avarua, Rarotonga, <u>Cook Islands</u>
E-Mail: <u>reservations@aquariusrarotonga.co.ck</u>

The newest of the Tepaki Group holdings on Rarotonga, the Aquarius is a bit of a mixed bag. 11 single/double rooms look out at the reef and ocean, all rooms feature king size or twin beds and a full bathroom. It is too bad they have fixed glass instead of sliders opening out to the deck, perhaps at some point they could change that situation. In a separate dormitory area are 12 bunk beds for the budget travelers, who share three communal bathrooms. The hotel is bright with high ceilings and teak floors. The indoor and outdoor restaurant appears to be well located with excellent views from a variety of tables around a small freshwater pool. Three meals a day are available in the Coral Club Bar & Grille. Costs for the 11 single/double rooms are NZ$75.00, while the dorm beds go for NZ$18.00 per day. These rates are listed as "onshore special" so rates will probably go up slightly in the future. Aquarius is a good option if you want to be near the airport, which is virtually across the street or if you are in Avarua to catch a connecting International flight or a flight to Aitutaki. You may want to grab a bunk for NZ$18.00 for the wait prior to the Los Angeles Air New Zealand flight that does not depart until nearly midnight.

Lambert's Lodgings, Ph. (682) 20-275, Fax. (682) 22-270
PO Box 245, Rarontonga, <u>Cook Islands</u>

Nestled between Pacific Resort and Muri Beach Club is Terry and Pu Lambert's budget accommodation in the heart of Muri Beach. There are two rooms with double beds and one room with two single beds in their home steps from the islands best beach. Terry and Pu are long time local residents and their home is ideal for couples and families. The home is close to restaurants shops as well as the round island bus line. A meal plan is available for NZ$15.00 per day for combination breakfast and dinner, or cook your own meals with provided kitchen facilities. All meals are served family style on their covered patio overlooking the lagoon. Room rental is NZ$35.00 per person per night, shower and toilet facilities are shared. You will be welcomed into the family by these two islanders and enjoy their special spot on the lagoon. I know, because I was lucky enough to stay with these two on one of my visits to the island and I highly recommend the spot.

Rau's Guesthouse, Ph. (682) 22-916, Fax. (682) 23-570
PO Box 438, Rarotonga, <u>Cook Islands</u>
Website: <u>www.rausguesthouse.co.ck</u>
Email: <u>atua@oyster.net.ck</u>

Next to the Avaavaroa Passage on the south side of Rarotonga, the family owned, Raus Guesthouse offers 3 double/twin rooms and two rooms containing two single beds. The property has a communal kitchen, lounge area and guest laundry. Affordable Internet access is available in the lounge area, which also features a TV and DVD. Raus favors a variety of island visitors and is said to be quieter than many of the backpacker lodgings. The guesthouse is within walking distance of Wigmore's Market, a well-stocked medium sized market and convenient to the round island bus. The yard features a barbeque for guest use and the beach is a short walk away. Rates are NZ$48.00/single, NZ$59.00 for double/twin and NZ$70.00 for triple, with a 5% discount for stays of seven or more days. The owner also has a separate spacious beach house, located in

Turoa. The self-contained beach cottage is just steps from the lagoon and suitable for up to four people. Rates are NZ$180.00 per day. Airport transfers are available for NZ$15.00 per person each way. Early check in and late check out are available and negotiable depending on occupancy.

Town House Backpackers, Ph. (682) 20-583
PO Box 2031, Rarotonga, Cook Islands
Website: www.cookislandsbackpackers.com
Email: info@cookislandsbackpackers.com

The newest budget lodging on Rarotonga is located in the heart of the residential district of Avarua. Proprietor "Auntie May" Kavana is a well-known local resident, known for her smile and warm personality. Rooms are basic, with a variety of options in a dormitory arrangement. Depending upon demand, beds can be moved and shuffled in a variety of arrangements. Two double beds, several single beds and several bunk beds can be arranged within the five rooms that make up the guesthouse sleeping area. There is a separate one-bedroom cottage that can sleep up to four adults located adjacent to the main building. The communal kitchen is open to all guests of the main building, the cottage has it's own kitchen, or eat at any of the dozen restaurants within walking distance of the property. Rates are NZ$35.00 per person for dormitory/shared rooms. Rates for private rooms are NZ$105.00 for single/double/triple, with the family cottage rents for NZ$140.00 for up to four people. Rates drop 20 to 30% for visits of four or more nights. Prices include airport transfers.

Where To Eat
on Rarotonga

Avarua Area

Trader Jack's Ph. 26-464 has a wide variety of seafood and charbroiled steaks. Prices range around NZ$25.00 for meals served on their deck overlooking Avarua harbor. Try the *Kati Kati* bar snacks at the U-shaped wooden bar and be sure to chat up Jack for tales of the island. Lunch is served Monday thru Saturday and dinners nightly. Look for daily specials on the specials chalkboard. Jack's offers a full range of appetizers, vegetarian meals and pizza. The bar and restaurant caters to a wide cross section of locals and visitors alike. Friday happy hour seems to feature most of the island businessmen and in fact I  was introduced to the Prime Minister during one of those Friday night happy hours. Jack's features live music most nights and the music blends well with the relaxed Polynesian atmosphere of the restaurant. Jack himself can usually be found anchoring the corner of the bar, lately his health has curtailed his merriment somewhat, but he still welcomes visitors to his watering hole.

Portofino Restaurant, Ph. 26-480 has been a favorite on the island for years. Back in 2003 Canadian Bruce McCartney had just taken over ownership of Portofino, it seems the restaurant is back up for sale, perhaps Bruce misses those hockey games on the television, or perhaps he is suffering from island fever. Let's hope whomever takes over the restaurant continues the tradition of top quality Italian cuisine for years to come. Portofino is on the main road at the east end of Avarua. Portofino has a full variety of Italian food as well as steaks, chops and the islands best pizza. Meals run in that NZ$25 to $30.00 range with pizzas costing from NZ$18.00 to $22.00 depending on toppings. There is indoor and outdoor seating near the fountain at Portofino's which serves dinner only six nights a week, closing Sunday. In addition to dining, Portofino offers pizza delivery or takeaway food from their walk up window. Call ahead and your pizza will be ready when you get there.

Tamarind House Restaurant & Bar Ph. 26-487 is arguably the finest restaurant in the Cook Islands, they certainly would get a lot of folks votes and have a strong following. Located about a mile East of the traffic circle in Avarua, they are open for breakfast from 9:00 AM and lunch from 11:30 AM every day but Monday. Tamarind House also serves morning coffee and afternoon teas all day. Prices are a bit on the stiff side but the atmosphere and sunset on the verandah make the prices justifiable. Come by for sunset happy hour on the verandah. Longtime local restaurant owner and chef, Sue Caruthers and her partner Robert Brown have created a first class establishment with varied and eclectic menu. The old heritage colonial house was originally the office of the Union Steamship Company fro
m 1909 until the mid 1980's, at which point it became the residence of the British Consul until the lease was sold to the two partners in 2003. The old residence was expanded and restored and officially opened in March of 2004. All was in order including extensive landscaping in time for the series of cyclones that passed through Rarotonga in February and March of 2005. The good news was the building itself suffered only

minimal damage and the gardens were replaced. A new Tamarind tree has been planted in the garden to replace the original tree that was destroyed by Cyclone Sally in 1987. Today the verandah looks out on the extensive gardens and waves breaking on the nearby reef. The view is only surpassed by the fine food served in the restaurant.

Try the Thai Fish Curry with lemon grass, basil and chilies served with rice and mint sambal for NZ$28.00. To insure the ambiance, children under five years of age are not allowed at this restaurant. Interested in more information, visit their web site at **www.tamarind.co.ck**

Raviz Restaurant, Ph. 22-279, those of you returning to the island will remember the spot as Ronnie's on the main road in town center of Avarua. Raviz in Rarotonga is a branch of a New Zealand chain with six locations throughout New Zealand. An extensive menu of classic Indian dishes are offered in a rather stark environment, with both inside and outside tables available. Friday and Saturday nights they feature a NZ$15.00 buffet. Dinner is served daily from 6:00 PM. Bring along your own wine, no corkage charge at Raviz. Lunch is available Monday thru Saturday from 11:00 to 2:30 PM. Takeaways can be phoned in and delivery is available on order of NZ$50.00 or more.

Staircase Restaurant & Bar, Ph. 22-254 on the main road near Jack's and Portofino serves dinners nightly from 6:30. Thursday night they host an island night performance (see island night chart) for particulars. The Staircase Island Night is the best bargain of the many island night performances that take place on Rarotonga. The cost is only $30.00 including dinner and entertainment. While I felt the meal was only fair, the combination was a big bargain when compared to the other island night venues. The bar is a popular spot and full of locals on Friday and Saturday nights.

In Avaruatown I favor three small cafes for that morning coffee or pastry fix. **Café Salsa Ph. 22-215, Blue Note Café Ph. 22-236, The Café Ph. 21-283,** all small storefront locations on the main road near the traffic circle. This is as close to Starbucks as you will find on Rarotonga, Café owner Neal Dearlove even roasts his own coffee. Over at Café Salsa try the eggs Benedict in the morning or a gingival pizza at lunch. I've always found the service to be a bit slow at the Blue Note, but there is always an Auckland newspaper on the rack to read as you await your meal on the porch of the old Banana Court building.

There are a host of fast food locations around Avarua, known locally as, "takeaways". Try the large hamburgers at **Palace Takeaway Ph. 21-438**, on the main road at Avitua Harbor, or **Ara Moana Fish N' Chips Ph. 21-250,** a few doors closer to the airport. They have a wide variety of food items besides the one their name implies and they also do a great hamburger. Try the *Ika Mata* marinated fish in coconut sauce, or if you are less adventurous the cooked fish is all locally caught. In Cooks Corner next to the bus depot, **Mae-Jo's Ph. 26-621** has a wide selection of sandwiches and surprisingly features both Mexican and Chinese food to eat on their patio or take home.

Arorangi & The West Coast

Windjammer Restaurant Ph. 23-950, on the main road, adjacent to the Crown Beach Resort. The indoor/outdoor Polynesian setting is quite dynamic. The indoor portion of the restaurant is one of the few air-conditioned eating-places on Rarotonga and a real oasis on a hot summers evening. Another contender for the crown as the finest restaurant in the Cook Islands, Windjammer offers elegant dining on the grounds of The Crown Point Resort. Windjammer is open for dinner only six-nights a week, closed on Tuesdays. Call ahead for reservations, as there is limited indoor seating in the restaurant.

Chef Daniel Forsyth and partner Maire Porter are Kiwis of Cook Island descent, well trained in New Zealand and masters of their craft. You will need to prepare yourself for a real treat, try the fresh seafood or either of the two vegetarian specials prepared nightly The menu is a-la-carte, with starters in the NZ$12.50 range and main courses in the NZ$25.00 to NZ$35.00. The author is not fond of restaurants attached to resorts, but in the case of Windjammer, I will make an exception.

Kikau Hut, Ph. 26-860 on the main road in the Black Rock area of Arorangi, Kikau House serves dinner from 6:00 P.M. Monday

thru Saturday, in a relaxed tropical setting with both indoor and outdoor seating. The food has a European flare, try the beef stroganoff or a rib-eye steak. There is no bar service at the Kikau Hut, but you can bring your own wine and Kathie and the staff will serve it to you. Figure to spend about NZ$25.00 to NZ$30.00 for your dinner entrée at Kikau Hut Restaurant

Saltwater Café Ph. 20-120 on the main road at the halfway point around the island in the village of Turoa, this small roadside café serves lunch Monday thru Friday and dinners on Tuesday, Wednesday and Thursdays. Owners Kerry and Ati are everpresent, and insure that your visit to their little restaurant is an enjoyable experience. Excellent home-cooked lunch specials attract a crowd. Call ahead for dinner reservations.

Alberto's Steakhouse Ph. 23-597 is in the same general area and located on the main road in Arorangi. Alberto's, as the name implies, has a variety of steaks as well as Italian specialties and nightly fish specials. Alberto's has a full bar and is one of the few restaurants on the island to offer a salad bar. Prices are in the NZ$25.00 to NZ$35.00 range for full meals and the restaurant is nicely appointed. The food was excellent but the drinks were a bit on the weak side. I shared an excellent Indonesian soup known as *thoo I pai*; very good and very spicy.

Tumunu Garden Bar and Restaurant Ph. 20-501 is just past the entrance to the Edgewater and on the same side of the road as Spaghetti House. Tumunu Garden specializes in fish and seafood. The atmosphere is excellent in the plantation style restaurant; they are open for dinners seven nights a week. Dinners range in the NZ$20.00 to NZ$30.00 range, try the Ahi tuna medium rare.

Right on The Beach Ph. 26-860 The old Manuia Beach Hotel restaurant has been rebuilt at least three times post cyclones over the years. The beachfront sand floor restaurant now begins its new life as the Right on the Beach Restaurant with a new name and a rebuilt building. The restaurant is fast becoming a favorite in Arorangi, so book well ahead especially for their popular island night buffet. Lunches are in the NZ$12.00 to NZ$20.00 range with dinners running in the NZ$25.00 to NZ$30.00 range.

South Coast Restaurants

Vaima Restaurant, Ph. 26-123, continuing around the main road to the south end of the island is my island favorite for a romantic evening. Sonny and Shannon go out of their way to see that you enjoy your dinner at Vaima. The restaurant serves an extensive menu of fish, Indian Roti's and curried meat, and Cajun flavored dishes as well as chicken and steaks cooked to order in an authentic Polynesian setting. Seating is both indoor and outdoor and the restaurant is situated right on a quiet stretch of beach. Vaima serves dinners six nights a week and is closed on Wednesdays. I enjoyed a fine rare rib eye steak and a couple of great Mai Tai's on my visit to Vaima. Try the killer garlic bread they serve to go with your Mai Tai. If you are a vegetarian, try the vegetarian curry. Check out the daily specials on their blackboard and tell them Papa Mike sent you.

The Pawpaw Patch, Ph. 27-189 at the Moana Sands Resort on the main road just before you reach Muri Beach on the South side of Rarotonga is a great place for a Sunday barbeque dinner, on an island where many restaurants are closed for the Sabbath, Megan and Took host a great night including light entertainment. The restaurant is open for breakfast from 7:30 to 10:00. No lunches, but reopens again for happy hour from 5-6:00 Monday thru Friday and Dinner is served from 6-10:00. Try the "Paw Paw Catch," fresh fish in Hollandaise sauce, served over onions, taro and coconut milk a yummy authentic Cook Island meal. Be sure and save room for the "Paw Paw Patch Brule," their signature desert. The barbeque night was NZ$25.00 and that included a choice of about half a dozen different desert items. The night included a local husband-wife-son string band that played during our meal. The barbeque was on the beach with tables set up for the night. The whole evening was quite enjoyable and well attended.

Yellow Hibiscus Ph. 20-002 This relative newcomer to the South Coast Restaurant scene has been well received as a reasonably priced alternative for breakfast or dinner. My last trip I stopped by for a drink with owner Grant Walker at his almost complete on site restaurant at Palm Grove Resort. Over a Fosters he explained his plans for the restaurant, a plan that has obviously blossomed into the Yellow Hibiscus. Way to go Grant, the breezy open-air restaurant is fast becoming one of the islands best bargains for breakfast and dinner. The

128

restaurant is closed for lunch and dinner reservations are suggested.

Maire Nui Café & Gardens Ph. 22-796 is more of a garden with an attached restaurant than just a restaurant. Breakfast, Lunch & Afternoon Tea are served from the thatched roof dining area on the Southwest corner of the island just before you reach Muri Beach. A slow paced meal served in, "true botanical bliss," or so they say. Organically grown fruits and vegetables along with homemade olive bread, cakes and muffins are served Monday thru Friday from 9:00 AM to 4:00 PM, try the cheesecake for a special treat. Maire Nui is a non-profit project, with all it's proceeds reinvested into its ongoing development. Be sure and check out the handcrafts on the wall, created by artisans on Penrhyn and Manihiki. If you have a few extra dollars, donations are accepted and will help towards continuing the gardens vision.

The Waterline Beach Bar & Grille Ph. 22-161 E-Mail: beachbar@waterline.co.ck You will have to keep your eyes peeled for this spot on the ocean side of the main road in

Arorangi. There is a sign on the main road and when you get to it follow the dirt lane past three homes all the way to the beach, where you  will find Chris & Akisi Musselle little restaurant tucked between a grove of coconut trees and the beach. There are currently only around a dozen oil lamp lit tables on the deck overlooking the sunset thought the palms, but the view and location are priceless. The menu is not large, half dozen main dishes with an emphasis on seafood, I enjoyed a delicious shrimp and scallop sauté with a warm coconut sauce over rice the night I was there. Chris is a proud Kiwi and former island charter boat captain, so expect to see a lot of nautical pieces in the décor of the restaurant. Waterline is open Tuesday thru Saturday from 6:00 PM. Arrive before 7:00 PM to insure you catch one of the most spectacular sunsets on the island.

Muri Beach

Sails Restaurant Ph. 27-349, which is adjacent to the sailing club, just as you get to Muri Beach and the adjacent lagoon. Look for a small sign on the right hand side and follow the lane to the lagoon; the restaurant will be on the right. I enjoyed the 'fish bites' as their fish and chips are referred to. They also serve a huge bowl of *iki mata* in a coconut sauce with local vegetables at lunch that is enough for two. The location, right on a deck overlooking the lagoon, insures that you will have an enjoyable meal. Lunches run in the NZ$10.00 to 15.00 range, with dinners in the NZ$20.00 to NZ$30.00 range.

The Flame Tree Restaurant Ph. 25-123, which is just past Sails and on the lagoon side of the main road. There have been some personnel changes in the past few years, but it is still one of my favorites on Rarotonga. Flame Tree is open for dinner 7 nights a week from 6:00 P.M. They are often crowded so it is best to phone ahead and make reservations.

Steffano's Italian Cuisine Ph. 22-232 on the lagoon side of the main road in Muri Beach, this tiny spot with but a few tables, is located at the front of a residence. Be sure and call ahead due to the limited tables and prepare yourself to be treated like family by Roberta and Steffano, who came to Rarotonga from

Milan, Italy back in 2000. All their pasta is hand made from premium quality durum flour and fresh island eggs. The same goes for their handmade sauces. Prices are a bit on the high side for pasta meals, with most traditional pasta and Ravioli dishes priced slightly higher than NZ$20.00. Try the scrupsuous Pasta al Gamberi with headless prawns served in a white wine, garlic, chili, capers and fresh tomatoes.

Miro's Café Ph. 20-693 is a new small café style restaurant with several shaded tables on a large verandah on the main road at the cut off to Muri Beach Club Resort. Two local island sisters opened the restaurant while I was on Rarotonga. They offer a varied menu of breakfast and lunch items and are open

seven days a week. Monday thru Thursday 8:00 AM until 5:30 PM, Friday & Saturday 8:00 AM until 7:30 PM and Sunday 8:00 AM until 3:00 PM I had a great cheeseburger served medium rare, a hard to find item in a region that leans on overcooking all meat items regardless of your request. The banana milkshake was large and full of the local sweet fruit. Required refreshment stop if you are staying in the Muri Beach area.

Bars

For those of you that relish the conversation that only occurs during happy hour at a local watering hole, I will now walk you around the island to a few of the locations that offer a cold beer and a friendly ear to the traveler. Since we are starting in Avarua, my first nominee is **Trader Jacks** on the waterfront at Avarua Harbor. While Jack's borders on being a bit on the yuppie side, Jack and the other sailors give the place a good nautical feel, the view of the harbor and the local ladies helped sell me on the place. The **Banana Court** geographically would have to be my next choice. The oldest watering hole in the South Pacific would get in strictly on seniority alone, but it still rocks on the weekends. Just around the corner from Trader Jack's is the **Whatever Bar & Grille** a relative newcomer to the waterfront in Avarua. A great deck overlooking the Avarua Harbor and North coast is quite enticing, but the trip down the spiral staircase requires your sensibilities in order. Keep the stairs in mind when it comes time to order that last drink. My third choice will turn a few heads, not that I care in the least; the **RSA** (Returning Servicemen's Association) would make few people's list of bars, maybe that's why I liked the unpretentious atmosphere at the place. The RSA is a male dominated environment for us golden oldies to celebrate past triumphs. Just to show that I am impartial, I would like to add the **Barefoot Bar** at the Pacific Resort in Muri Beach. Just 'cause I can't afford to stay there, doesn't mean I can't have a drink there! The fact that the bar sits directly on the lagoon helps, it is just a gorgeous location and a great place to people watch on a warm afternoon. You really should join the **Sportfishing Club**, if you are planning on spending more than ten days on the island. $20.00 in dues will make you a member and allow you to buy a $25.00 ten-drink card, which works out to very cheap drinking. The club is a great way to meet a huge group of locals, some of which actually go fishing from time to time. Tell them Papa Mike sent you, maybe if I drum up enough members, they'll give me an honorary membership. I will close my list with an un-official bar, the deck at the **Paradise Inn**, for most nights you will find me on the deck at the Paradise Inn for my version of happy hour. I can't invite you all over, because it is for guests only, but if you wander back and find me out back with my *chilli bin* and my Mt. Gay, I will be happy to buy you a drink. As I always say, enjoy the island and support your local bartender.

Aitutaki Atoll

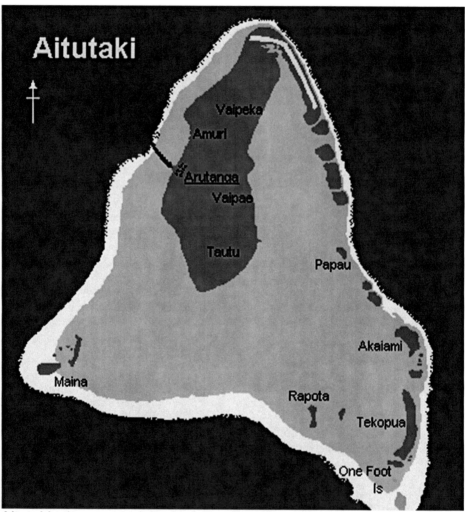

Aitutaki, the most visited of the Cook's outer islands, is often compared to French Polynesia's Bora Bora The two coral surrounded islands feature lagoons that are neck and neck in any lagoon derby. I consider a trip to Aitutaki to be a must on any trip to the Cook Islands. There are four daily flights from

Rarotonga, as well as a day trip to the island, so the island is the most convenient and easily reached of the chain's out-islands.

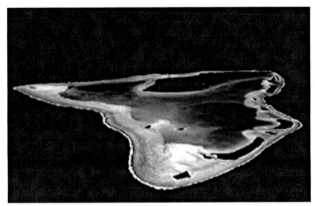

Since the lagoon is the primary reason for visiting Aitutaki, most activities center on the lagoon. Besides the lagoon cruises, deep-sea fishing, and scuba diving, many visitors enjoy the pleasure of snorkeling or kayaking from the shores of their accommodation. As on Rarotonga, island night cultural dancing is performed at various locations on the island and is indicated in the, **Where To Eat** section below. Renting a motor scooter and discovering the island or just lying on the white sand beach in front of your accommodation, Aitutaki offers the visitor a slower pace of life than Rarotonga, with one of the world's most beautiful lagoons thrown in for a bonus.

Those of you who are fans of the US television show *Survivor* will recall Aitutaki, as it has twice hosted the popular shows season long melodrama. The show caused quite a stir on the island, a brief economic upturn and many locals who felt the show, with its inherent hindrance to daily life during shooting, to be a major pain. As a result of the anticipated arrivals from America, several small beach developments were constructed, some of which are now for sale. It seems that the twenty-five million television viewers would rather sit on the couch with a beer than travel to some far off South Sea location. The anticipated rush from Stateside has never materialized and most locals are quite content with that result.

Getting There

The primary method of getting to Aitutaki is via air; contact **Air Rarotonga Ph. 22-208** in Rarotonga. They also have a local office in Aitutaki, on the main road north of Arutanga, their number is **Ph. 31-888**. The airport is located at least 7km. from most of the accommodations, so you will need to obtain transfers from your hotel or guesthouse. Look for Willie and his bus at the airport, he will take you to your hotel for NZ$10.00 and at that time, you can make arrangements for him to come by and pick you up when you leave. Willie has a quick wit and is dependable, an ex-rugby player, he knows what is happening on the island, so be sure and ask questions as he delivers you to your hotel. Tell him "Papa Mike" says hi.

The secondary source of getting to Aitutaki is the inter-island freighter, and if you have read my section on inter-island travel, you will already have my opinion of this means of transportation. With this in mind and if you still insist, contact **Tiao Shipping Ph. 24-905** and attempt to ascertain if a voyage to Aitutaki is anticipated within your travel schedule. It is possible to take the ship over and return on the plane. Just keep in mind that the ship rarely sails on the first indicated date of departure.

If you have made up your mind that you do want to visit Aitutaki, it is usually less expensive to try and purchase a combination air and hotel package. Besides the airline itself, which offers the day excursion and packages, there are several travel agents back in Rarotonga that offer these packages. Try **Island Hopper Vacations Ph. 23-026, Fax. 23-027, or E-mail: vacation@islandhopper.co.ck,** or **Jetsave Travel Ph. 29-907, Fax. 28-807, or E-mail: Jetsave@cooks.co.ck,** or **Tipani Tours Ph. 25-266, Fax. 23-266, or E-Mail:**

Tours@Tipani.co.ck. Shop around for the best deals as all vary in price.

In addition to trips to Aitutaki, these consolidators can put together multi-island packages involving the southern group islands. One of my suggestions would be to visit Aitutaki and Atiu, as this combination is available without a return to Rarotonga, unlike most others, which require a return and switching of planes in Rarotonga.

Getting Around

There is no public transportation on Aitutaki and it is quite a way from the airport to your accommodation. Transfers from and to the airport, may or may not be provided, depending on where you are staying. If you need transport to and from your hotel, there is a bus available **(see getting there).** Once you arrive at your hotel, simply indicate to the desk your intention to rent a car or scooter and they can make arrangements. Your car or scooter will then be delivered to your hotel. In some cases, upper class accommodations have rentals available on site. Prices are higher than Rarotonga. I suppose, based on supply and demand. If you are renting for several days you can sometimes negotiate a discount. If you wish to deal direct, contact **Rino's Rentals Ph. 31-197** or **Swiss Rentals Ph. 31-600**. They are on the main road north of Arutanga, within walking distance of each other and close to most of the smaller hotels on that section of the island. They rent bicycles for NZ$5.00 per day, scooters for NZ$25.00 per day and cars for about NZ$70.00 per day. If you are over in the Ootu Beach area, **Ranginui's Retreat Ph. 31-657** has a few scooters that rent for the bargain price of NZ$20.00 a day, around the corner from Ranginui's, **Popooara Rentals, Ph. 31-553, E-Mail: fishing@aitutaki.net.ck** have 11 rental cars and 40 rental scooters over at their location near Ootu beach adjacent to the popular Boat Shed Bar & Grille and their Popooara Villas.

Rates for cars are NZ$65.00 per day and scooters go for NZ$25.00.

Things To Do

The first thing is off to the lagoon. Lagoon cruises are available in a number of varieties, from several providers. The oldest firm is **Bishop's Lagoon Cruises Ph. 31-009. E-Mail: bishopcruz@aitutaki.net.ck** They have been doing this for ages and have a fleet of boats far larger than the Cook Islands Navy. Does the oldest do the best job, or are they resting on the backsides of their reputation? I met visitors that had both opinions, so it is your choice as to the current state of lagoon cruises. The "newer" upstarts are, **Teking Lagoon Cruises Ph. 31-582 E-Mail: teking@aitutaki.net.ck** which is run by the husband wife team of Teariki and Teina George on a 24-foot pontoon boat and they specialize in smaller groups with a maximum of 10 people per tour. They offer a wide range of tours, including a half-day tour leaving at 9:00 AM or at 1:00 PM. Try their Champagne Breakfast Tour to Maina *Motu*. In addition to the tours, Teking offers private charters and water taxi service. They can whisk you to a *Motu* for the day and then return to pick you up at a prearranged time. Be sure and take along a lunch and plenty of fluids for the day. **Kia Orana Cruises 31-442 E-Mail: kcruise@aitutaki.net.ck** is another smaller operator, run by Andrew Katu, a long time captain at Bishop's and is now on his own with a small boat that can also accommodate up to ten people. The smaller boat and the fact that Andrew reverses the order of his island cruise from the other operator's guarantees smaller crowds on the islands. All operators provide transfers, snorkeling equipment and lunch as part of the cruise. Teking and Kia Orana both avoid the traffic and crowds at One Foot Island, providing lunch on their own private *Motu,* providing a much more intimate tour.

Exploring the island on a rented motor scooter is always my own personal favorite way of locating restaurants, watering holes, markets and hidden beaches on any given island. Pick up a *Jason's Cook Islands* map available at your hotel and take off on your own self-orchestrated adventure. On Aitutaki, I found a little used dirt road off the south road from Nikaupara to Tautu; it meanders down lush fields to a couple of hidden beaches on the southern tip of the island. The sign on the road indicates Marae, but it is past Marae on the way to the religious village. Take along some insect repellant and a sense of adventure, as it really doesn't indicate a road on the map, just a trail. I can assure you that it is passable by scooter and I saw locals on scooters at the beach, and that always indicates to me that it is acceptable to travel the route. Once you arrive you will find the beach is really not much of a swimming beach but you can cool off and enjoy the view across the lagoon prior to remounting and ascending the trail.

A second spot is a secluded sunny beach just past the runway at the airport on the northern tip of the island. This is a good swimming beach, but offers no shade. Watch out for loose sand as you approach and you may want to park close to the road to avoid bogging down on your scooter. Take along a cooler and water and watch the planes land from the perspective of a warm lagoon.

Most hotels offer basic snorkeling equipment as part of the room charge, some have a nominal fee for use of this equipment, while others at the top end of the accommodation chain offer not only snorkeling, but windsurfing and sea kayaks in the cost of accommodation. Check in to what your hotel offers. If you want to go beyond what they offer and rent a sea kayak, go to **Samade Water Activities, Ph. 31-526** on Ootu beach, adjacent to the restaurant of the same name. Take the road to Black Pearl Resort next to the airport runway. Take this road all the way to the end and then branch off to the right to the restaurant. Time your activities to coincide with lunch or dinner to enjoy the restaurant. They are located at the end of the lagoon and when I visited the mosquitoes were taking no prisoners. A bottle of repellant is suggested. The cost of a kayak is NZ$10.00 per hour or NZ$24.00 for the day, call ahead to see what the availability looks like, or arrive early to insure all are not rented. Near Samade's, **Ranginui's Retreat Ph. 31-657** offers kayak rentals as well as operating Wet & Wild Adventure Tours, specializing in wake boarding and tube riding in the lagoon off of Ootu Beach as well as offering lagoon taxi service and lagoon cruises. Call ahead to find out what is happening during your stay on island to get wet and wild!

For those who wish to go beyond snorkeling at the lagoon off of the hotel beach, there is excellent scuba diving offered by Neil Mitchell at his dive shop, **Aitutaki Scuba, Ph. 31-103, Fax. 31-310. E-mail: scuba@aitutaki.net.ck** Neil offers four day PADI and NAUI certification courses as well as offering a variety of dive options in and around the lagoon on Aitutaki. The new guy in town is Onu Hewitt, his **Bubbles Below Ph. 31-537** offers both scuba diving and fishing tours. Costs vary depending on your needs, for more information visit Onu's extensive website at **www.diveaitutaki.com** or E-Mail him at **bubblesbelow@aitutaki.net.ck**

Like Rarotonga, Aitutaki has its own version of **island night**, the famous Maori singing and dance celebration. While the Aitutaki version differs slightly from the former, some say the less polished dance troupes of Aitutaki are more traditional and less glamorous. You will have to judge for yourself, but all island nights are a wondrous event to the visitor and well worth attending. **Samade's (Ph. 31-526)** hosts island night on Tuesdays, while Friday night is island night at **Pacific Resort (Ph. 31-720) If** you are on Aitutaki on a Saturday; the Aitutaki Lagoon Resort has island night on that day.

There is, by what would have to be a literal interpretation, a **Golf Course** on Aitutaki. It is nine holes in length, adjacent to the "Aitutaki International Airport" and features a prevailing breeze that encourages "grounders" for best results. The golf course has been on the island for a great deal of time, but has evaded any renovation or major capital expansion plans during that time. In years past the airport runway was considered part of the course and divots were extracted from it's coral strip. In recent years the increase in air traffic has deemed the runway out of bounds, much to the applause of Air Rarotonga and the demise of golfers island wide. The golf course at Aitutaki is the only one I am aware of without a phone, but somehow if you let your hotel know you are a crazy golfer and want to play golf, they will somehow locate someone that knows about these things and arrange you a tee time. Green fees are NZ$ 20.00 and rental clubs are available for NZ$ 10.00 As you can imagine, a golf club without a phone, lacks in the locker room amenities, but you can at least amaze friends at cocktail parties with your tale of golf on Aitutaki.

If you are one of those types who like to hike to the highest point on the island and I know there are many of you out there, you have the opportunity to hike to the top of 410 ft. Mt. Maunga Pu, which is best to do early in the morning or late in the afternoon, for a sunrise or sunset view of the entire island. The trailhead is across from the Paradise Cove Hotel (which is next to Puffy's that sell, very cold Heineken beer for $3.00). I never did get past Puffy's, but I understand the sunset was "awesome," at least that was what I was told by female backpacker she was munching on trail mix as I stumbled out of Puffy's. I love nature almost as much as happy hour. If the walk up to the top of that mountain has not tired you out and you yearn for another hike, try the Aitutaki walkabout, on the road between Reureu and Tatu. Take a right at the Marae cutoff past Café Topuna if you are coming from Reureu, look for the signs. Don't ask me where it goes, I couldn't find that backpacker again to find out, but I'm sure it was also "awesome" mate.

If hiking is not on your vacation itinerary you can contact the folks at **Aitutaki Discovery Safari Tours Ph. 31-757 E-Mail: safari@aitutaki.net.ck** and sign up for their four-wheel jeep tour of the island. The tour is similar to the safari tour on Rarotonga, led by locals and packed full of information on the culture and history of the island. You will visit the two highest points on the island for a fantastic view of the lagoon, visit the sacred *marae* sites where your guide will explain the legends of Aitutaki. At the end of the tour island refreshments are served in traditional fashion on banana leaves, you will relax and your tour guide Ngaakitai will answer any questions you may have. Cost of the Discovery Safari Tour is NZ$55.00/$28.00 for adult/child. In addition to the jeep tour Ngaakitai, offers a walkabout tour of the island and in season night crab hunts

If it is your first visit to Aitutaki, and you have completed your obligatory lagoon cruise you will likely yearn to see what is available above water level. Contact **Nane & Chloe's Tropical Tours Ph. 31-248** for a circle island tour that will allow you to explore the sights in the comfort of their van. These two gorgeous young ladies, will show you and tell you of the above water attractions of Aitutaki. The price for the tour is NZ$35.00 which includes transfers to and from your lodging. This is a great introduction to the island and will expose you to the various attractions allowing you to concentrate on what interests you.

There are several operators offering deep sea fishing or fishing within the lagoon. For the serious fisherman try **Aitutaki Sea**

Charters Ph. 31-695, or **Clive Baxter Ph. 31-025** they both offer four to five hour trips outside the reef. Figure on spending around NZ$100.00 per person for these trips. **Barry Anderson Ph. 31-492** offers full day trips inside and outside the reef for NZ$150/NZ$180 single/double. If you want to stay closer to dry land, **Tuono's Ph. 31-562**, offers trips to the reef for NZ$40.00/NZ $70.00 for single/double in there small open boats. No indication as to disposition of any fish caught, but on Rarotonga the fish are sometimes the property of the boat owner and sometimes shared with the fisherman. You may want to ask before your dinner departs with the captain.

Places To Stay

There is a full range of accommodations on Aitutaki, from resorts all the way to basic backpacker lodgings. Listed below from expensive to shoestring are the vast majority of accommodations available at the present time on the island. The comments are obviously subjective and represent the authors opinion, as brilliant or short sighted as you may judge that opinion. As always, properties change hands, and some of the best become far less than what they might have been on my brief visit. If your opinion varies, please feel free to E-mail me with updates at the address listed in the front of the book. There are not enough accommodation choices on the island to break them down by price category, but I have listed them starting with the high end and descending to the least expensive accommodations on the island. All rates are per day. In addition to the lodgings listed, individual villas and bungalows are sometimes available, as well as homes and apartments for longer term rentals. If you wish to view a sample of the available semi-long term rentals, contact Nane & Chloe's Tropical Tours 31-248, and they will be happy to pick you up as part of their Circle Island Tour and point out units that can be rented, while showing you the island.

Aitutaki Lagoon Resort & Spa, Ph. (682) 31-201 Fax (682) 31-202 PO Box 202, Aitutaki, <u>Cook Islands</u>
Website: <u>www.aitutakilagoonresort.com/</u>
E-Mail: <u>info@aitutakilagoonresort.co.ck</u>

The owners of the Rarotongan Beach Resort recently purchased the Pearl Beach Resort. I anticipate that this change will result in a higher level of service, as their hotel in Rarotonga is one of the best run in the South Pacific. The hotel is situated on its own small island and is accessible by footbridge from the main island. The hotel contains spotless pristine grounds and the rooms are quite lavish with individual decks that overlook the gardens and lagoon. The individual bungalows feature both air conditioning and ceiling fans to insure your comfort. Use of native woods and woven cloth accentuate the island feel of the bungalows, with the vaulted ceilings making the units appear even larger than their ample size. The resort features two restaurants and bars, a large teak decked swimming pool and the lagoon is directly accessible to the resort's complimentary canoes, kayaks and windsurfers. Lagoon cruises leave their dock daily and cruises, car or scooter rentals, scuba diving and deep sea diving can be arranged by contacting the friendly staff at the front desk. I was quite impressed by the hotel itself but one of my pet peeves revolves around staff being dressed in the same "island togs" so they look like lagoon guides in Disneyland's Adventureland. What is it with that? The staff meets all the flights and bestows a lei and coconut drink, complete with umbrella and straw to each new arrival before shuttling them off to paradise. The rates are NZ$335.00 single/double with one queen size bed in the three garden units that adjoin the main building. The sixteen deluxe garden bungalows go for NZ$595.00 single/double and contain one queen and one single bed in each unit. The 9 deluxe *lagoon view* bungalows are similar to the garden view units and offer the same features for NZ$760.00. Thus the view of the lagoon and a deck near it are valued at NZ$165.00, which is probably fine to Robin Leach, but seems a bit stiff to those of us of more modest means. There are five beachfront suites, which are genuinely spectacular, complete with a king size and single bed and large deck overlooking the full extent of the lagoon. At NZ$975.00, they offer most a once in a lifetime chance to experience paradise like few will ever enjoy it. The seven over water bungalows rent for NZ$1,1195.00, a rather numbing amount for most, but I think all of these rates reflect rack rates and most bookings are made as part of package tours and reflect a discount from these rates, so look at the consolidators websites shown in the, **Other Resources**, section of **Planning Your Trip**, and see if you can't do a bit better.

Pacific Resort Aitutaki, Ph. (682) 31-720 Fax (682) 31-719
PO Box 90, Aitutaki, Cook Islands
Website: www.aitutaki.pacificresort.com
E-mail: reserations.ait@pacific resort.co.ck
For quite some time the Pearl Beach Resort has had the distinction of being the only luxury resort on Aitutaki, but that all changed in recent years with the completion of the Pacific Resort Aitutaki. The two differ in approaches, with the Pacific Resort choosing to understate the grandeur of their hotel to those passing by on the main road. But there is no mistaking the elegance of the resort once you pass the front desk. The resort has been molded to the shape of the property, with the restaurant/bar and pool utilizing the raised point of land to its advantage to terrace down to the water's edge. There are thirteen beachfront bungalows clustered to the right of the pool all with large decks and direct beach access. The six beachfront suites offer a large deck, outdoor shower and direct access to a private section of beach. The three beachfront villas offer a separate living area as well as sleeping suite with an outdoor shower. All bungalows/villas and suites offer more amenities than I have room to list. All have both air-conditioning and ceiling fans, bathrooms are floor to ceiling marble with slab

145

marble countertops. Located in each unit is granite wet bar, T.V., and DVD Player. All classes of accommodation feature king size beds. Each unit is hand constructed using native Polynesian Architecture and construction, with thatched roofs and hand woven ceilings. In short the Pacific Resort has created a terrific boutique hotel and it is hands down my choice for favorite high-end resort on Aitutaki. Rates are NZ$795.00 single/double and NZ$895.00 triple for a beachfront bungalow. The beachfront suites are NZ1060.00 for single/double, NZ$1160.00 for triple. Prices for the beachfront villas are NZ1470.00 for up to four persons. Prices include full breakfast and airport transfers. As you might have figured, the front desk can help you schedule activities and rent scooters or cars. Children under 12 are free when sharing with adults.

Samade on the Beach, Ph. (682) 31-526
PO Box 75, Aitutaki, Cook Islands
Website: www.samadebeach.com
E-Mail: samade@aitutaki.net.ck

These 12 lagoon side bungalows are an outgrowth of the popular Samade's Restaurant, Bar and watersports rentals. The location is on the South end of Ootu Beach near Rangiuris and the Aitutaki Lagoon Resort. These pricey units are well located on a good swimming beach and the adjacent restaurant is convenient and serves a reasonably priced menu of three meals a day. Samade's location at the far end of the lagoon is a favorite location of those pesky mossies, but depending on the wind and whether they pose little threat to your enjoyment of the beautiful lagoon. All bungalows are fully self-contained, air-conditioned with ceiling fans, refrigerators, coffee service, televisions and cd changer. The bungalows are serviced daily with complimentary use of Kayaks, beach loungers and a beach volleyball court in case Karch Kiraly is staying in the adjacent bungalow. It's a short walk to board a lagoon tour and rental cars, scooters and activities can be arranged with management.

Rates are a rather healthy NZ$275/NZ$300 for single/double. These prices include Continental Breakfast, flower lei greeting and tropical juice on arrival. Airport transfers to and from the nearby airport are also included in the prices.

Etu Moana Beach Villas Ph. (682) 31-051, Fax (682) 31-459
PO Box 123, Aitutaki, <u>Cook Islands</u>
Website: <u>www.etumoana.com</u>
E-Mail: <u>onthebeach@etumoana.com</u>

Recently completed in late 2003, these traditional thatch roof villas are located on a large parcel, which allows for great privacy in any of the eight villas. All units face the lagoon and are finished in top of the line finishes, granite counters, hardwood floors and teak furniture. This is a great location for those upward mobile executives looking to escape the hustle and bustle of work and the urban jungle, be it Sidney, Paris, New York or Johannesburg. For those who can afford the tariff, they will not be disappointed with the seclusion and ambiance of Etu Moana. Lounge around the pool in teak loungers, enjoying the complimentary breakfast or refreshments at the self-service honor bar. When you are ready to partake in nature, jump in one of the complimentary Kayak and paddle out to the reef, for an afternoon of snorkeling or maybe hop on one of Etu Moana's bicycles for a leisurely trip down the island for a cold Foster's in town. If the effort of pedaling is beyond your desires, ask at the desk and they will arrange for car or scooter rental. For a minimal charge you can hit the Internet, to check the Nasdaq and decide if you will eventually need to return to the civilized lifestyle that seems so far in your past. Rates start at NZ$425.00 per villa with a maximum of three per villa. The third guest is an extra $100.00, which is a steal if you bring along Selma Hayak for the vacation with the spouse. Rates drop a smidgen if you stay more than four days. Airport transfers are included, but Selma Hayak's wardrobe is extra. Book early to avoid disappointment, Tripadvisor.com lists Etu Moana as the 7th best bargain in the world, whatever that means.

Tamanu Beach Resort, Ph. (682) 31-810, Fax (682) 31-816
PO Box 102, Aitutaki, <u>Cook Islands</u>
Website: <u>www.aretamanu.com</u>
E-mail: <u>info@tamanubeach.com</u>

A couple of years ago Are Tamanu merged with Manea Sunset Resort, creating what is now known as Tamanu Beach Resort. The combination creates an interesting mix of island themed luxury studio bungalows on the Are Tamanu side and a selection of one-bedroom suites over at the Manea property. Both lodgings were highly regarded before the merger and will remain that way as far as I can see into the future. The on-site Vaka Bar and Grille, is located near the pool and offers tasty meals with plenty of ambiance.

The twenty-two individual luxury bungalows at Tamanu are located on the main road north of Amuri. Each individual luxury bungalow retains a view of the lagoon, with six units on either side of a central walk that leads to the restaurant bar and swimming pool. Each thatched roof bungalow or *Are*, as they are called in the islands, has a separate bathroom with shower, hair dryer, kitchen with breakfast bar and outdoor deck. Each unit has a king-size bed, refrigerator and freezer, a gas cooker as well as a microwave oven. In addition each unit comes equipped with air conditioning, ceiling fans and insect screens. Complimentary tropical breakfasts, use of their bicycles and use of kayak, snorkel and fins is included in room rates. When you return from a swim or a bike ride, take advantage the outdoor barbecue to cook up your meal. Owners Michael and Kuraona Henry and their staff are onsite daily to make any tour arrangements you may require and to assure you that you receive the pampering that will make your stay a memorable visit. Rates are NZ$400 per night single/double and add

NZ$85.00 for a third bed. The end beachfront unit is the honeymoon suite with a double sized deck and additional windows with views of the lagoon. This unit rents for NZ$451.00 per night. The on site bar and restaurant is open daily and there is a barbecue for guests on Sundays.

Maina Sunset Resort, Ph. (682) 31-511, Fax (682) 31-611
PO Box 34, Aitutaki, Cook Islands
Website: www.soltel.co.ck
E-mail: Solomon@oyster.net.ck

At the southern end of the main island, Maina Sunset Resort is situated across from the road from the lagoon amongst a grove of trees. The eight studio and four one-bedroom units are situated around a central courtyard surrounding the swimming pool. Each unit contains a queen size and single bed, separate toilet with shower, cooking facilities, with refrigerator. The units are fully screened and contain ceiling fans. In front of each unit is a small verandah that overlooks the pool area and is equipped with a table and chairs. At the time of my visit the on site restaurant was not complete but completion was anticipated soon. Some snacks were available at the front desk, where the staff would be happy to assist you with tours or rental vehicles. Rates are NZ$160.00 per day single/double for the studio units and NZ$195.00 for the one-bedroom units, with discounts for longer stays. You can work out a package price with their sister property the Reefcomber Sunset Beach Resort on Rarotonga.

Aitutaki Beach Villas, Ph. (682) 31-181
PO Box 41, Aitutaki, Cook Islands
Website: www.aitutakibeachvillas.com
E-Mail: tini@oyster.net.ck

On the popular north coast of Aitutaki, these four raised cottages occupy a secluded hideaway amongst a grove of coconut palms adjacent to a white sand beach. Where swimming and snorkeling are virtually at your doorstep. These four thatched roof bungalows are tastefully furnished, fully self-contained and within walking distance of several restaurants and a small store. Each comes equipped with a queen sized bed and a single bed for up to three adults. All four boast a covered patio with chairs overlooking the garden or lagoon, which faces the sunset. There is a shared kayak, for your pleasure and airport transfers are included in the rental. Paradise does have it's price as rates start at NZ$180.00 per night for garden view cottages and runt to NZ$250.00 per night for absolute beachfront units. There is a three-day minimum stay required, but if you stay for a week you pay for only six days. Just think of that sunset over the lagoon from your deck and check your credit card limit.

Ranginui's Retreat, Ph. (682) 31-657, Fax (682) 31-658
PO Box 8, Aitutaki, <u>Cook Islands</u>
Website: <u>www.ranginuis.com</u>
E-Mail: <u>ranginui@aitutaki.net.ck</u>

This property is only a stone's throw from the Black Pearl resort on Ootu Beach and features lagoon front double bungalows directly adjacent to the lagoon. The day I visited was feeding day for the mosquitoes and they were out in force. I found not a sole around and beat a hasty retreat, but before leaving I took a look around and was impressed by the location and proximity of the lagoon. I am quite sure that a little repellant and/or a shift in the wind could render the retreat a little slice of paradise. Besides, there is something wonderful about looking across the lagoon at the Black Pearl Resort and knowing that you are enjoying the same sunset for a fraction of the cost. Rates at Ranginui's are NZ$110.00/$120.00/$150.00 for single/double/triple The units are self-contained, but lack a kitchen sink, so cooking is somewhat limited on the furnished hot plate. Each unit has a queen-sized bed. The wooden beachfront deck is equipped with a table and chairs and there are restaurants within walking distance of the retreat.

Inano Beach Bungalows, Ph. (682) 31-758, Fax (682) 31-553
PO Box 48, Aitutaki, Cook Islands
Website: www.inanobeach.com
E-Mail: inano@aitutaki.net.ck

These seven relatively new and spacious bungalows are nestled in the Southern corner of Inano Beach, on a secluded white sandy beach within walking distance of three restaurants. This is an excellent mid-priced lodging option, with one absolute beachfront bungalow, five lagoon and garden view bungalows and one larger family sized (up to 4 people) bungalow. All bungalows feature a large palm covered porch and lagoon views. Standard bungalows have a queen-sized bed, while the family bungalow has an extra single bed in a separate room. All bungalows are quite spacious, fully self-contained with open plan kitchens and ensuite baths. Rates are NZ$130.00 for lagoon view, NZ$160.00 for beachfront and NZ$170.00 for the family bungalow. These units were hand built with pride by the owners, Moyeau and Veia, who live on site and are happy to assist you with activities and tours during your stay on Aitutaki.

Popoara Ocean Breeze Villas, Ph./Fax (682) 31-553
PO Box 4, Aitutaki, Cook Islands
Website: www.popoara.com
E-Mail: fishing@aitutaki.net.ck

In the same general area as Inano Beach Bungalows, the addition of Popoara Villas a couple of years ago, has added another interesting small intimate villa complex to this popular area of the island. Four smallish open plan studios with covered patios offer lagoon views, ceramic tile floors, and either a queen-sized bed or twin beds with overhead fans and a fully equipped kitchen. The on site Boat Shed Restaurant is popular with visitors and locals alike. Owners Allen and Maria are on site daily and more than happy to help you with planning tours. Car and scooter rental is available on site and families are invited at Popooara. There is a no smoking policy within these villas, something that I, as a non-smoker can appreciate. The villas rent for NZ$185.00 per day and the rate includes transfers to and from the nearby airport.

Sunny Beach Lodge, Ph. (682) 31-446, Fax (682) 31-446
PO Box 94, Aitutaki, Cook Islands
E-mail: sunnybeach@aitutaki.net.ck

On the main road just south of the Pacific Resort, the Sunny Beach Lodge has five self-contained units just above a sandy swimming beach amongst a coconut grove. This low-key property has clean spacious rooms in a motel fashion with a walkway the full length of the five units. Along the walk are plastic chairs to allow you to sit outside your unit. The rather large units have ceiling fans, are fully screened and each has a clean small kitchen with a table and chair. Floors are all tiled and the open ceilings give the units a very open feeling. My only complaint was that the shower was raised above the room floor nearly nine inches, a bit scary for us more senior members of the travel writer fraternity. Rates are NZ$80.00/$90.00/$100.00 for single/double and triple, with discounts for longer stays. As always rental bikes and cars, as well as tours can be arranged from the front desk. Just ask. Four of the five units have a double and single bed, while the fifth is a double room with a queen size bed.

Rino's Beach Bungalows, Ph. 31-197 Fax (682) 31-559
PO Box 140, Aitutaki, Cook Islands
Website: www.rinosaitutaki.com
E-Mail: rinos@aitutaki.net.ck

On the main road just south of Sunny Beach Lodge Rhino's has  long been a fixture on Aitutaki. There are eight studio bungalows at the main location with another four units in an apartment configuration about 2 km. north of the beach property. All units are self-contained, with ceiling fans, and refrigerators, the apartment units are across the road and away from the beach so you will need to walk back or ride your scooter back to the sister property to swim. Rates at Rino's for the four garden view bungalows are NZ$111.00 for single/double the two beachfront bungalows are NZ$169.00 for single/double. The two beachfront deluxe bungalows are NZ$221.00 for single/double. Rates on the four apartment units are NZ$120.00 for single/double. Rino's has a good snorkeling beach adjacent to the bungalows and they have their own on site rental cars, jeeps, scooters and bikes.

Gina's Garden Lodges, Phone/Fax (682) 31-058
PO Box 10, Aitutaki, Cook Islands
Website: www.ginasaitutaki.com
E-mail: queen@aitutaki.net.ck

Gina's is a good spot for families, with each of the four units accommodating up to four adults or three adults and two children. While away from the lagoon it is only a ten-minute walk to Tatu Village and shops or you can swim or picnic at Tatu Landing. Each self-contained lodge is spacious, has two fans, refrigerator and cooking facilities. Use of the communal barbecue area, pool and sundeck is included in the room rate. The Clarke family, owners of Gina's have a substantial beach house on neighboring Akaiami Island, with use of the house and white sand beach exclusive to guests at Gina's. The Lodge has it's own boat to ferry you to their beach house. Rates at Gina's are NZ$75.00/NZ$120.00 for single/double. A third adult is $30.00, while children 0-15 years old are $20.00 each per day. Rental scooters and bikes are available and tours can be arranged.

Paratrooper Motel, Ph. (682) 31-563, Fax (682) 31-523
PO Box 73, Aitutaki, Cook Islands

As the name implies the place is run by an ex-New Zealand paratrooper Geoffrey Roi. Geoffrey offers heavily discounted budget accommodations on an island of above average costs. He is not accredited with the tourism board and after all those years of military service, I think he does not like having policy dictated to him by a higher authority. The official rate on the two one-bedroom apartments is NZ$60.00 single/double and includes full cooking facilities. Stay eight nights or more and he will reduce the rate down to NZ$35.00 per night. The three two-bedroom family units are only NZ$60.00 per night for six or more nights. As you can see Geoffrey likes extended stays and less turn over. All rates are negotiable so if things are slow you can call up the old paratrooper and make him a deal he can't refuse.

Paradise Cove Guesthouse, Ph. (682) 31-218, Fax (682) 31-456
PO Box 64, Aitutaki, Cook Islands
Website: www.paradisecove.co.ck
E-mail: mtl@aitutaki.net.ck

Long a mainstay of budget accommodation on Aitutaki, the Paradise Cove is located on the main road north of Arutanga not far from the airport. The least expensive rooms are the five rooms in the main house which rent for NZ$35.00/NZ$45.00 for single/double with shared bath. In addition to these units there are six small huts that rent for NZ$45.00/NZ$55.00 for single/double with shared toilet and shower facilities. The units are quite small with most of the interior space being taken up by the large bed, refrigerator and small table and chair. The six beachfront self-contained bungalows are larger and have a deck directly on the lagoon. These units rent for a non-budget figure of NZ$250.00 per night, but are comparable to other beachfront lodging on Aitutaki. Paradise Cove has large grounds as well as a nice beach for swimming and snorkeling. Puffy's Restaurant is right next-door and offers good meals at reasonable prices.

Vaikoa Units, Ph. (682) 31-145, Fax (682) 31-145
PO Box 71, Aitutaki, Cook Islands
E-Mail: vaikoa@aitutaki.net.ck

On the main road just north of Arutanga, this seven unit complex is a bit rundown and in need of a repair. Each unit comes with a queen size bed as well as a single bed. The units are screened and come equipped with ceiling fans. Each unit has a small kitchen as well as a small patio area. The beach and lagoon are directly adjacent to the property and offer the main reason for staying at Vaikoa. The rates at NZ$55.00/S75.00/$85.00 per night, per night which is reasonable and the rates drop some if you stay for a week. Hopefully the owners will spruce up things soon and make the units a little brighter and easier on the eye. In recent years the owners did put in several beachfront bungalows that are superior to the older units, rates for these units are NZ$110/$130.00 for single/double, with discounts for stays beyond one week.

Matriki Beach Huts, Ph./Fax (682) 31-564
PO Box 32, Aitutaki, Cook Islands
Website: www.matriki.com
E-Mail: matriki@aitutataki.net.ck

Look for the sign on the left hand side of the main road as you travel from the airport towards Arutanga, make a right and follow the two track all the way to the beach, that is where you will find this tiny four-unit budget tiki hut styled lodging. I had heard rave reviews and was anxious to meet Fred and Kristene, the managers of this tiny oasis tucked amongst a coconut grove and only steps away from the beach. This Canadian couple is energetic, enthusiastic and has created a unique lodging on the North side of Aitutaki. Fred is a master diver and both of the two are water sports enthusiasts and former movie stunt persons.

Matriki was completed too late for the last guidebook, but is a welcome addition to the new book. Nestled in a coconut grove, just steps from the lagoon on the northeast coast not far from the airport. Matriki offers personalized service and great prices for those willing to hike to the bathroom in the middle of the night, avoiding the nocturnal land crabs with flashlight in hand, No heated showers or room service, just friendly folks and a great spot on the beach. Kristene and hubby Fred are the managers and will go out of their way to insure that any activity you wish to accomplish on Aitutaki is available with a minimum of fuss. Rates for the three beachfront units are as follows, there are two units referred to as the "treehouse units" which consist of an upstairs unit with kitchen facilities, refrigerator, dining table and screened double bed. The highlight of this unit is the private deck overlooking the lagoon. The downstairs unit is much the same, with an extra single bed for triples or families. My favorite is the "beach hut" unit, with a thatched roof, secluded deck overlooking the beach. The kitchen is bare minimum. The treehouse units share an outdoor shower, while the beach hut has a separate outside shower. All three of these units share a single flush toilet, which is in a separate building and requires that midnight stroll if the need arises. The final unit is a large "garden unit" which is slightly behind the beachfront units and about thirty yards from the beach. The garden unit is fully self-contained with it's own indoor shower and toilet. This unit has a double and fold down single bed if needed. Current rates are NZ$55.00/NZ$70.00 single/double for the beach hut. The garden unit is NZ$60.00/NZ$80.00/NZ$97.50 for single/double/triple. The two treehouse units rent for NZ$55.00/NZ$75.00. In the lower treehouse unit add NZ$22.50 for a third person. Fair warning, all units are self-servicing, so don't look around for the maid. Linens and towels are provided by management, so just think of making your own bed as adding to the adventure of staying at Matriki. There is a small convenience store and a couple of restaurants in the general vicinity of Matriki Beach Huts

Toms Beach Cottages, Ph. (682) 31-051 Fax (682) 31-409
PO Box 51 Aitutaki, Cook Islands
Website: www.ck/aitutaki/tomsbeach
E-Mail: papatoms@aitutaki.net.ck

Well my first advise to you is not to ask for Tom when you arrive, 'cause Tom is the proprietors last name, just ask for Taraota or Mimau, the Polynesian couple that operates this seven unit guesthouse, which is next to a sports field and tucked amongst a grove of trees on the main road between the airport and the wharf in Arutanga. They will be happy to welcome you to their very attractively priced guesthouse on the beach. The seven comfortable rooms are in the old family home, a few steps from the beach, lagoon, a mini-mart and an Internet Café. Rooms in the old family home are a bit worn, but a good value for beachfront on Aitutaki. Tom's even have a reasonably priced self-contained beachfront honeymoon bungalow, with a private kitchen and hot shower. Not exactly Etu Moana, but you can fund your IRA with the price difference. Rates are NZ$32.00/ NZ$48.00 for single and double, with triples at NZ$60.00. That honeymoon bungalow is a very reasonable NZ$84/NZ$98.00 for single/double with another $12.00 if you brought along Selma, (see Etu Moana listing for relevance). Airport transfers are NZ$8.00 per person each way, which is only fair, considering the great pricing at Toms. This is an excellent choice for budget lodging on Aitutaki, tell them Papa Mike sent you and you will receive a 10% discount on a stay of more than seven days. Don't worry if you don't mention Papa Mike you still get the discount.

Amuri Guesthouse, Ph. (682) 31-749, Fax (682) 31-231, PO Box 6, Aitutaki, <u>Cook Islands</u>
Website: <u>www.ck/aitutaki/amuri</u>
E-Mail: <u>Amuri lodges@hotmail.com</u>

If you are in search of inexpensive basic lodging on Aitutaki, Amuri is an interesting option. The warm friendly owners Nga and Mariati Tom have refurbished the old family home located in a garden setting, into six double bedrooms, three of which have double beds, two with a double and single bed and one with two twin beds. The rooms share two full baths and a large dining area with cooking facilities. There is no air-conditioning, but each room has his and hers fans to keep you reasonably comfortable. The location of Amuri is just north of the main village of Arutanga, within walking distance of a white sand beach, snorkeling, mini-mart and Internet café. Rates are reasonable at NZ$40.00/$70.00/$90.00 for single/double/triple. Students and visitors staying for more than seven days, receive a 10 percent discount. Aren't we all students of human nature? Couple the favorable rates with free airport transfers and you have a very reasonably priced trip to Aitutaki. Have a large family or group? You can rent the whole guesthouse for NZ$350.00 per night, subject to availability. Children and families are always welcome at Amuri.

Josie's Beach Lodge, Ph. (682) 31-659
O'otu Beach, Aitutaki, <u>Cook Islands</u>r.

Located directly across the causeway from the prestigious Aitutaki Lagoon Resort, this popular budget property is directly on the waterfront, just down from Samade's Restaurant. There are seven very basic rooms at Josie's with either two twin beds or one double bed and have in room fans and insect screens. Baths are shared as is the communal kitchen and laundry facilities. Josie's is an adult only facility, with no children under 12 allowed. Rates are reasonable at NZ$28.00/$38.00/$50.00 for single/double/triple

These last two lodgings are in a class of their own, the Robinson Crusoe class, for if you choose either one of the two you will have an island to yourself. Both are located on the unoccupied *motu* of Akaiami, which was the original refueling terminal location for the TEAL flying boats back in the fifties. You will be five miles from the occupied island, on a pristine beach overlooking one of the world's most beautiful lagoons, a location fit for a king.

Gina's Beach Lodge Ph. (682) 31-058
Akaiami Motu, Aitutaki, Cook Islands
Website: www.ginasaitutaki.com
E-Mail: queen@aitutaki.net.ck

Robinson Crusoe can stay for NZ$180.00, but if he brings along his faithful servant Friday the rate is NZ300.00 for a double. Children 12 to 15 are an additional NZ$60.00, while 8 to 11 year olds get by for NZ$20.00 per night. Children under 8 years of age are free. The lodge is nestled amongst the palm trees with three studio type rooms and separate cooking, toilet and shower facilities. The lodge is fully furnished, with a verandah/porch that looks out through the palms to the lagoon. A generator provides electricity and the stove is gas. The kitchen has a refrigerator, you just need to bring along all groceries and snorkeling equipment. Transport to and from the "mainland" is provided by the owner, as are airport transfers.

Akaiami Lodge
PO Box 3, Aitutaki <u>Cook Islands</u>
Website: <u>www.coralroute.com</u>
E-Mail: <u>mamaruru@aitutaki.net.ck</u>

There is no television, no radio, no videos, no gizmos of any kind to detract you from enjoying the crescent-shaped, white sand beach at your doorstep, or so states the Akaiami Lodge Website. The lodge building is constructed from handcrafted local timber, and is true to the original design of the old TEAL terminal building, which back in the fifties was visited by movie stars the likes of John Wayne and Cary Grant as their flying boat was serviced and refueled. The large open plan main room houses the present day restored lodge, solar power and batteries provide electricity for the lights, ceiling fans and the fully equipped kitchen. A separate building houses the bathroom and hot water shower. Eat inside or enjoy the covered seating area and barbeque. You will be picked up at the airport by the lodge staff, driven by local stores where the staff will advise you as to your food and supply purchases and then driven to the lodges dock on the main island. You will then be ferried to Akaiami *motu,* a fifteen-minute boat ride away. Upon departure you will be returned to the main island and dropped of at the airport for your return to Rarotonga. All of this is included in the daily rate of NZ$600.00 for one or two guests, additional guests are NZ$50.00 each up to six people. Prices include the use of the lodges two-person kayak so just bring along your swim suit your fishing pole and snorkeling gear for the vacation of a lifetime just you and Robinson Crusoe.

Where to Eat

The choices on Aitutaki are somewhat limited when compared to Rarotonga, but there is an adequate selection of restaurants . If you are planning to dine at one of the accommodations that takes outside guests, always call ahead early in the afternoon or the day ahead if you will be gone on a lagoon cruise that day. Since most lodging is self-catering, which means it comes with cooking facilities, you may want to prepare some of your own meals. The main source of groceries on island is **Maina Traders Ph. 31-055** which has a fairly good selection of the basics. They are located on the main road in Arutanga. For fruits and vegetables try **Tauono's Ph. 31-562,** which is just off of the main road in Arutanga and also the location of the popular restaurant of the same name which offers lunches and dinners (by reservation). Stop by for spot of English afternoon tea, between 3 to 5 PM on Mondays, Wednesday or Fridays. The fruit stand is open from 10:00 to 5:00 weekdays.

Next to Paradise Cove is **Puffy's Bar, Restaurant and Takeaways, Ph. 31-317**, which serves lunches from 11-2 daily and Sunday 12-3. Dinners are served from 6-10 daily and some nights there is light entertainment. There are some enclosed tables, but the majority of the seating is in an open-air covered patio. The fish and chips is only NZ$7.50 with two huge pieces of fish. I enjoyed Puffy's and would recommend it for lunches or dinners if an informal setting meets your needs. The adjacent bar stays open until 12:00 depending upon demand and beer is NZ$3.00 each.

If you have a hankering for Chinese food, you can order it to go or sit at the few outside tables at **Mae-Jo's Ph. 31-820** on the main road in Amuri. Its pretty basic Chinese, but it's hard to expect much more than that on an island out in the middle of the South Pacific. Mae-Jo's is closed on Sundays.

I saw no nuns; blue or otherwise, but the **Blue Nun Café & Bar, Ph. 31-604** on the waterfront in Arutanga is another fine choice for breakfast, lunch and dinner. Once again it is open-air and located in the large warehouse building next to the dock on the left hand side as you face the dock. The extensive menu offers everything up to and including a T-bone steak for NZ$26.00 as well as fish, chicken and pork entrees. Call ahead to find out about their island nights schedule. This restaurant is a good choice for coffee or a beer in the morning or afternoon of a lazy day on Aitutaki. The bar is a popular spot at sunset and the Blue Nun has island night performances on Wednesday and Saturday nights in season.

On the Tatu village road, east of Arutanga sits the **Café Tupuna Ph. 31-678,** which has long been known for its island cuisine. The restaurant is outside on a patio, with cooling island breezes in a relaxed unpretentious setting. Great food and a great setting, it is one of my all-time favorite restaurants, even if it is a little out of the way. Tupuna is only open for dinners and you will need to call ahead for reservations.

Over on Ootu beach is **Samade Restaurant & Bar, Ph. 31-526,** which is open for breakfast, lunch and dinner daily. Sunday is barbeque day at Samade, popular with visitors and locals alike, come early for a good table. The cost of Sunday barbeque is NZ$22.50 served buffet style. The restaurant is beachside and the bar is jumping most Friday nights for "Beach Party Night." The food is Polynesian and the atmosphere is casual. There are kayak rentals next door and many people spend the day on the beach at Samade, combining lunch, dinner and a sunburn. In the evening the mosquitoes are prevalent in the area and you may want to take along some repellant if you plan on staying into the evening. Food is a bit pricey, but the beach and setting makes up for the cost difference. Tuesday is "island night" at Samade, so call ahead if you plan on attending.

Not far from Samade's is the **Boat Shed Bar & Grille Ph. 31-479** Located at Popoura Ocean Breeze Villas in the Ootu beach area. This is a relatively new restaurant, with table service inside, on the deck and at three tables in the shade of several pandanus trees. The restaurant is on the corner of the lagoon and receives a constant trade wind breeze off the Pacific. The nautical themed dining area is full of varnished wood and offers lunch from 12:00 to 5:00 and a substantial dinner menu from 6:00 to 9:30 PM daily. The open-air feel has attracted a following of visitors and locals alike since it's opening a couple of years ago. Lunches including sandwiches, salads and fish and chips run from NZ$8.50 to $15.00. A more extensive dinner menu includes a variety of grilled items as well as coconut baked prawns and grilled sirloin. The house specialty is a three-course seafood combination for two at NZ$75.00. The attached bar offers the usual libations, starting with a variety of beers for NZ$4.00.

The islands newest eatery is **Kuru Café Ph. 31-110** Over in the  Ootu beach triangle near the "Y" intersection of the road that splits, the left branch leading to Aitutaki Beach Resort and Josie's Beach cottages and the right branch which leads to Samade. Look for poster boards sign on the right side of the road advertising specials. Kuru is only open for breakfast and lunch, but the service is good, the restaurant is clean and the prices reasonable. Seating is on the patio or in the octagonal shaped dining area. You will see lots of local Aitutakian artists work on their walls, buy some and take it home to Kansas, your friends will think you won the *Survivor* television show. I had the pancakes, which come topped with fresh local bananas, lathered in maple syrup and sprinkled with powdered sugar.

Equal to any "grand slam" breakfast at Denny's. The restaurant had been open less than a month when I was there, but a steady stream of customers came through the door. One of the few locations for real coffee on Aitutaki and a great place to sit and chat with Trina or fellow customers. Trina and Steve are great hosts, try the Salt & Pepper Calamari for lunch, it comes highly recommended and is pictured below. Hours are 7:00 AM to 4:00 PM Daily, order in or takeaway.

If you are looking for a good place to sip a beer and chat about the one that got away, you can't do much better than the **Aitutaki Game Fishing Club, Ph. 31-379** near the Blue Nun at the wharf in Arutanga. Another popular watering hole, with a happy hour every day that ends in a "y" is **Ru's Beach Bar Ph. 31-201** the only problem with the place is the location over on Akitua Island at the Aitutaki Lagoon Resort, but if you have a boat or are staying nearby Ootu Beach, stops in for a cold Cook Islands Lager.

Mangaia

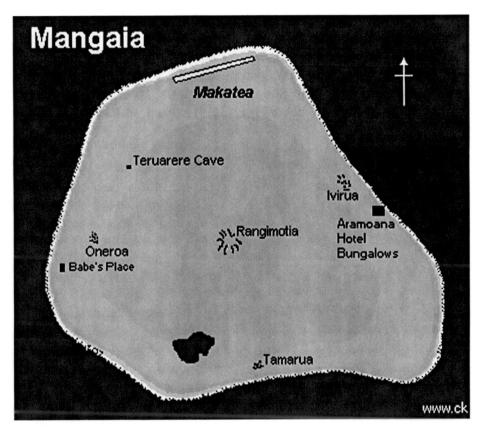

Mangaia sits 140 miles southeast of Rarotonga, all by itself, kind of the Rodney Dangerfield of the Cook Islands. The island that can't seem to get any respect and, although an island nearly as large as Rarotonga, an island that lacks a secure economic basis. Back in the 1980's the government experimented with pineapple production, but the logistics of trying to ferry the fruit in small boats from the dock on Mangaia, to a waiting freighter offshore and then continue onward to Rarotonga where the process had to be repeated, just amounted to too much handling. At times the fruit sat on the dock while the freighter waited for suitable weather. As the fruit began to rot on the docks, Mangaia's economy slipped into the dumps and many islanders left for greener pastures. Today the remaining thousand islanders produce pineapples for their own use as well as their other sustenance crops of Papaya *Paw Paws*, Breadfruit *kuru*, and reputedly the finest *Taro* grown in the Cook Islands. The flavorful Mangian pineapple is now grown for local consumption only and life on Mangaia has returned to the relaxed pace that it enjoyed prior to the great pineapple boom.

Mangaia is said to be the oldest island in the South Pacific, with a layer of *makatea* limestone coral that is sixteen to nineteen million years old. This layer of coral has created numerous caves on the island and exploring these caves is one of the main reasons people come to Mangaia. The caves all occur on private property, so you will need to arrange for tours with the people at your accommodation. In addition to the caves, many travel to Mangaia to relax and enjoy island life, as it existed fifty years ago on small islands in the South Pacific. For those who enjoy bird watching, the *Tanga'eo* bird is unique to Mangaia and easy to spot with its bright yellow coloring. Once thought to be extinct, it is currently enjoying a nice recovery on the island. Sight seeing on a rented scooter is always great fun, exploring at your own pace as you circle the island. There is even a road to the highest point on the island Mt. Rangiomotia. Check to see if it has been graded recently as during the rainy season it becomes quite rutted. If you would rather walk than ride, the island has numerous roads and hiking trails for both beginner and advanced alike.

Visit Mangaia and you will be treated to an island that few get to see, some very special geologic conditions and typical Cook Islands hospitality. Not bad for an island that can't seem to get any respect.

Getting There

The vast majority of visitors fly from Rarotonga on **Air Rarotonga Ph. 34-888** (Mangaia) **Ph. 22-888** (Rarotonga); there are four weekly flights on Monday, Wednesday, Friday and Saturday. If you are planning on visiting other islands in the southern group you will want to purchase a multi island package, as this will result in a cost savings. See the **Getting Around** section in the front of this book for information. Island freighters do make trips to Mangaia from Rarotonga. Please read the section in the front of this book referring to Inter-Island freighters before considering this method of travel.

Getting Around

All accommodations on the island can arrange for or provide rental scooters or bicycles. Costs vary but you can figure to pay around NZ$30.00 a day for a scooter and NZ$10.00 a day for a mountain bike. If you wish to rent a car or truck, let your accommodation know ahead of time so that they can try to arrange a rental, as there are few rental cars and trucks on the island. The cost will be around NZ$60.00 per day. There is no public transportation on Mangaia, so the only alternative is to hoof it. Hitchhiking is frowned upon, and frankly, you may never see a vehicle headed your way for a couple of hours, so as I said, walking is the alternative.

Things To Do

Cave tours and island tours, can be arranged from your place of accommodation. **Tuara George Ph. 34-105** leads tours of the Teruarere Cave, the cost is NZ$25.00 per person. In addition **Clarke's Tours** offers caving tours for NZ$30.00 per person, in addition to cave tours they offer an island tour for NZ$50.00 per person.

Over on the other side of the island **Jan Kristensson Ph. 34-278** owner of Ara Moana Bungalows offers a wide variety of tours to their guests as well as outsiders. A guided 3 to 4 hour island tour is NZ$50.00, with the abbreviated two hour tour costing NZ$30.00. A three-hour *makatea* and cave tour is NZ$45.00 per person. There are two separate cave tours; the *Teruatere* cave tour is NZ$25.00 and takes one hour, while the *Toraapuru* cave tour is NZ$20.00 and takes about a half hour. Jan also offers ocean fishing tours in a boat for NZ$50.00 and reef fishing trips for NZ$15.00

.

You can rent scooters by contacting the desk at Babe's Place or direct from Ara Moana Bungalows. If you like you can rent a scooter direct from **Mini Dean Ph. 34-341, or 34-319 evenings.** In addition to the above, **Moana Rentals Ph. 34-307,** has a limited number of new motorbikes in the village of Tavaenga. Your rental will include the cost of delivery and pick up, so the first day is usually more expensive than subsequent days, in my case one day was NZ$35.00, while the two day rate was only NZ$50.00. Rates at Ara Moana and Moana rentals should be approximately the same.

Places To Stay

On a small island, the choices are somewhat limited. In the case of Mangaia, not only are they limited, but the three major choices are each very different types of accommodations. The Ara Moana Bungalows are located in the village of Ivirua on the windward side of the island. They are bungalows made of natural materials and the location of the accommodation is away and unto itself. Babe's Place is on the outskirts of Oneroa. The units are basic block construction, with the four connected units in a motel type arrangement. The Mangaia Lodge is located in an old Victorian home, on the upper end of Oneroa, next to the hospital. So these are your choices, at least from a style standpoint. Amenities and costs are discussed below under each individual establishment's listing.

Ara Moana Bungalows, Ph. 34-278 Fax. 34-279
Ivirua, Mangaia, <u>Cook Islands</u>
Website: <u>www.aramoana.com</u>
E-mail: <u>holiday@aramoana.com</u>

Jan and Tu Kristensson's eight bungalows are tucked into a corner of *makatea* below the village of Ivirua and not far from the beach. The huts are of Polynesian architecture and have been in operation for about twelve years. As Jan leads you on a tour of his property, it does not take long to realize that he and his lovely wife have spent a great deal of time and effort to create the grounds and buildings of Ara Moana. The ocean is less than fifty meters from the bungalows and there is a path down to a small nearby beach.

They have three types of units on site. There are two budget bungalows of rather tiny proportions; I refer to these as the, "Billy Barty Suites", these two rent for NZ$60.00 single and NZ$80.00 double. They share a separate toilet facility. The double bed is at the far end of the tiny bungalow, so if the person in the back has to go to the toilet...well you get the picture. To the rates above add a meal plan of NZ$35.00 for breakfast and dinner or NZ$45.00 for three meals. These budget units are for those backpacker types that can get by on the minimum.

The six standard bungalows offer a substantial step up from the budget units. Besides ceiling fans and full screens, the standard unit has a full bath with shower and a porch large enough to sit on and enjoy. Rates are NZ$115/135 single/double. To these rates add a meal plan of NZ$35.00 for breakfast/dinner or NZ$45.00 for three meals. Prices above include all airport transfers.

If you have read the section concerning what to do on the island, you will already know the many tours offered by Jan and of his genuine concern that you enjoy your time on Mangaia. Meals at Ara Moana are served in their open-air restaurant/bar which doubles as a meeting place for guests and a showcase for the string band entertainment that Jan often features in the evenings. Jan's wife Tu, a native Mangaian, prepares all meals at Ara Moana and is reputed to be an excellent cook. If you can't finish your meal, just look around for Ruff, the housedog; maybe he can help you finish your *taro*. I can assure you that Jan and Tu will do all they can to make sure that your visit to Mangaia is enjoyable.

Babe's Place, Ph. 34-092 Fax 34-078
Oneroa, Mangaia, Cook Islands
E-mail: mangaia@babesplace.co.ck

Babe's is the second option for accommodations on Mangaia and is located in the lower or Kaumata portion of Oneroa, just on the outskirts of town. The main building has two bedrooms that sleep up to four people each, with shared bath, while a separate motel wing has four units with a double and single bed in each unit and a full bath including a shower. These four units each have covered patios with table, chair and lounge. The grounds are large and well manicured, with native flowers in abundance. I was surprised to find that the units were not screened and did not have ceiling fans, although my unit contained a mosquito net. I find the things to be of little use to someone who turns over in his sleep as much as I do. In addition, during my stay the shower was down to a dribble and made shampooing of hair a struggle. In spite of these two minor complaints, I enjoyed my stay at Babe's; in no small part due to the kind and thoughtful care of Ura and Mata my hostesses. When I mentioned the fan problem they promptly found me a fan for my room. All prices at Babe's include all three meals served in the large open kitchen or the covered deck alongside the kitchen. Meals were quite enjoyable, with the local fish dinner being my favorite, there was ample food and the local fruit was great. Pricing at Babe's is quite simple; single is NZ$75.00 while double is NZ$120.00 and as mentioned these prices included all three meals. As mentioned in previous sections, Ura or Mata can arrange tours and call to have a rental car or scooter delivered to your door. Prices above include all airport transfers.

Mangaia Lodge, Ph. 34-324 Fax. 34-239
Oneroa, Mangaia, <u>Cook Islands</u>

Next to the hospital in the upper portion of Oneroa, Mangaia Lodge is an older Victorian style home converted to a lodge at some time in the past. The owner Torotoru Piiti, explained about the hot water and how he was waiting for a part from New Zealand. I explained that in this climate I felt the need for hot water was minimal and not a major problem. He assured me the part would be here soon and he would once again have a supply of hot water. He then led me through the lodge and the three bedrooms that he rents as he explained the pricing for his rooms. He stated that his rates were NZ$25.00 per person per night, but only if they made the reservation direct and not through a travel agent. I thought about my travel agent back home and had a chuckle. As if he could find Mangaia, much less the Lodge on Mangaia. But, you are hereby warned, book direct.

There are three bedrooms at the lodge; two have three single beds while a third has a double bed. Shared toilet facilities are in a separate building at the back of the hotel and as stated rates are NZ$25.00 per person. Meals are not included but can be arranged in advance.

Other Accommodations

Some local islanders will take people in on a home stay type situation. Enquire at the **Mangaia Tourist Office, P.O. Box 10 Oneroa, Mangaia, <u>Cook Islands</u> Ph. 34-289, Fax. 34-238** the office is in Oneroa on the right at the bottom of the hill.

Where to Eat

The only outside restaurant on the island is **Auraka Restaurant and Bar Ph. 34-281 or 34-007**. The restaurant is located at the front of Allan Tuara's bakery, near the hospital, in the upper portion of Oneroa, and is only open part time, based on supply and demand. So you will need to call him and find out what the current situation is and what food he has available. Allan makes great bread and rolls and will even sell you ice cold beer, which to many constitutes a meal. At least you wont starve on the island.

Both Babe's and the Ara Moana prepare meals for their guests and will accept casual dinners. Call ahead early and ask for reservations at either location. There are no major markets on Manguia and you may want to bring some food with you from Rarotonga. Keep in mind you are limited to 16 kilos per person on Air Rarotonga and gauge your food and luggage accordingly. There are a variety of small stores in each of the three villages, which carry a variety of snacks and cold drinks.

Manihiki

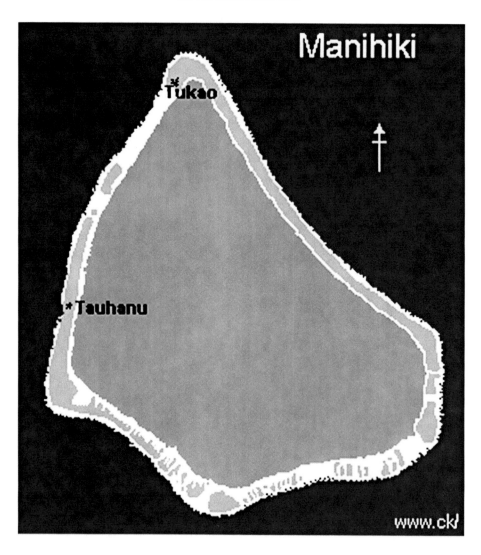

From the air, Manihiki resembles its number one cash crop, for the 40 small islands appear to be a string of pearls and black pearls are what drive the economy of Manihiki. The islands surround the two and one half mile lagoon that is the source of

the pearls and life in the two villages of Tukao and Tauhanu. Manihiki sits on top of an underwater mountain that rises thousands of feet from the ocean floor. The island is low lying, with the highest point being just a few feet above sea level. The small *motus* that ring the island are covered with palm trees. Some varieties of fruit are grown on the island and neighboring Rakahanga, which is only thirty miles north of Manihiki. Curiously, there are no bananas grown on the island, for the soil is too sandy. Water, as is the case on most low-lying islands, is a valuable commodity and large plastic cisterns are used to capture rainwater for drinking and bathing. Electricity is available from 6 to 12, both A.M. and P.M., so you have lights and appliances in the morning and again in the evening, but not in the afternoon. Go fishing or snorkeling in the afternoon, you don't need electricity
.

Most activities and the livelihood of the approximately 500 Manihikans revolve around the pearl industry. Tours of a pearl farm can be arranged. Just talk to the locals when you arrive on the island. As is the case everywhere you travel in the Cook's, the locals are always happy to accommodate visitors. There is much talk about the over farming of the lagoon for oysters and many say the lagoon has reached or exceeded the safe yield of pearls. The government is in the process of surveying and assessing the safe yield of the lagoon; hopefully the balance of protecting the lagoon will take precedence over the maximum dollar output in pearls. A trip to Manihiki will allow the visitor to experience Polynesian life as it was fifty years ago, to go back in time to a simple life on an atoll in the South Pacific. The lagoon itself is simply spectacular and besides the pearl farms is home to a wide variety of fish and shellfish. When I visited Tukao, I could lie in bed and listen to the fish splashing about in the lagoon next to my room and during the day could gather *paua* (clams) in the shallow water in front of my lodging.

Getting There

The few visitors that do visit Manihiki fly from Rarotonga on **Air Rarotonga Ph. 43-888** (Manihiki) **Ph. 22-888** (Rarotonga); there are but two weekly flights on Tuesday and Thursday. Flight time to Manihiki is approximately four hours. If you are planning on visiting other islands by plane, you will want to purchase a multi island package, as this will result in a cost savings. See the **Getting Around** section in the front of this book for information. Island freighters do make occasional trips to Manihiki from Rarotonga. Please read the section in the front of this book referring to Inter-Island freighters before considering this method of travel.

Getting Around

There is no public transportation on Manihiki, so the only alternative is to walk. Both of the villages on Manihiki are on small islands, so everything is within walking distance. To travel from Tukao to Tauhunu you will need to take a boat and it takes roughly twenty minutes to travel either direction. Ask about transportation at any of the village's small shops or inquire where you are staying. They will take you or find someone who can take you to the other village.

Things To Do

While Manihiki may be a quiet peaceful island, there are a variety of activities that may be undertaken to occupy your time on the island. You can contact **Jetsave Travel Ph. 27-707** in Rarotonga which can arrange an island package that includes air fare, accommodation and activities like a visit to a pearl farm, fishing trips, motu tours or snorkeling trips. If you prefer, you can wait until you reach the island. Introduce yourself to an islander and they will be only to happy to refer you to their neighbor the pearl farmer, or to a friend who can arrange a fishing trip. All these activities are of nominal cost, figure around NZ$30.00 for most activities and add NZ$20.00 if they include a meal.

A stay on Manihiki itself is an activity the likes of which you will probably never encounter in your life. Savor it and experience a simple life in this unique environment. For a short time, enjoy island life surrounded by a lagoon that is truly one of the earth's natural wonders. Besides, think of all the stories you will have to tell when you return to Kansas.

Places To Stay

There are no hotels on the island and tourism is in its infancy on Manihiki. Below are the few options available, keep in mind showers will not be heated and the water is to be used conservatively. Also keep in mind pricing below includes all three meals. You may want to bring along some snacks from Rarotonga, as there are no grocery stores on Manihiki, but there are some small shops that offer limited snacks and soft drinks.

Manihiki Lagoon Villas, Phone & Fax, 43-122
Tahhunu, Manihiki Island, Cook Islands
Website: www.manikikilagoonvillas.com
E-Mail: nancio@oyster.net.ck

There are two self-contained one-bedroom bungalows, which overhang the lagoon. Each is equipped with a queen size and single bed. Rates are set for NZ$110/200 for single/double with a triple costing an additional NZ$50.00. Cooked meals are included and provided by owners Kora and Nancy. Electricity is on between 6 and 12 A.M. and P.M on Manihiki. Explore one or more of Manihiki's 40 uninhabited *motus* or visit an operational plack pearl farm. There are plenty of fish to be caught in the local waters. The owners have a nearby guesthouse, rates at the guesthouse are NZ$80.00 per person, including meals.

Manihiki Guesthouse
Tukao, Manihiki Island, <u>Cook Islands</u>
Website: <u>www.jetsave.co.ck/manihiki_island.htm</u>
E-mail: <u>jetsave@cooks.co.ck</u>

Lodging is in a three-bedroom home in the village of Tukao. Your hosts Jane and Bernardino Kaina will welcome you into their home and according to Jetsave Travel; Jane is an excellent cook and will prepare all three meals for you in her kitchen. Water is not heated so showers are at room temperature, which can be refreshing. Reservations for the guesthouse need to be made through **Jetsave in Rarotonga Ph. 27-707**, which can also arrange tour activities on the island. Rates are NZ$82.00 for single/double/triple, add a child for NZ$45.00 per night

Manihiki Lagoon Lookout
Tukao, Manihiki, <u>Cook Islands</u>
Website: <u>www.jetsave.co.ck/manihiki_island.htm</u>
E-mail: <u>jetsave@cooks.co.ck</u>

The lookout is a pole house on the water's edge in the village of Tukao. Facilities are limited at this accommodation. Besides the electricity that only runs part of the day, the shower facilities consist of a bucket of water next to the house. The good news is there is an inside toilet. Your host Helen Muir will prepare all three meals and promises to make your visit unforgettable. Bookings are made through **Jetsave Travel Ph. 27-707** in Rarotonga; so contact them for reservations and availability. In addition to this accommodation, Jetsave can help arrange various tours on the island.

The only other accommodations would have to be a home stay. Talk to the tourist board in Avarua before you leave Rarotonga. They may have some names or you can talk to the various pastors of churches if you arrive on Manihiki without accommodation.

Places To Eat

As there are no restaurants on Manihiki, you will likely be eating all three of your meals at the guesthouse where you are staying. There are some small shops on the island where you can purchase some snacks, but supplies are limited and selection will be dependent on how close you are to a freighter visit during your stay. You will want to bring along some of your favorite packaged snacks to Manihiki, as the shops have only basic items.

Mauke

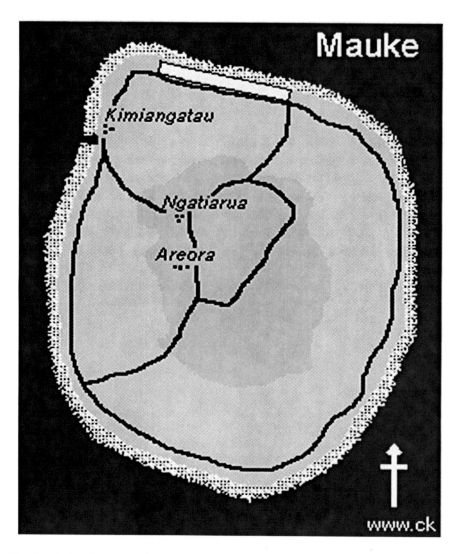

Tucked in the southeastern corner of the Cook Island chain, Mauke is similar in a lot of ways to neighboring Mitiaro and Atiu. All three have those nasty *makatea* coral formations and like Mitiaro and Mangaia, Mauke Island has numerous caves. The island is essentially flat, but full of lush tropical vegetation. The population on Mauke is approximately 600 and the vast majority of islanders live in the northern half of the island, in the villages of Areora, Ngatiarua and Kirniangatau. The best beaches are on the south side of the island, though swimming is limited due to the barrier reef. The lagoons are large enough to allow a cooling dip or two while sunbathing and the large coral formations offer shade from the sun.

The flower leis of *maire* produced on Mauke are exported to Hawaii, so chances are if you received lei upon arrival in Hawaii, it very likely was created on Mauke. The lei industry is thriving on Mauke and it provides jobs, as well as economic benefits to the islanders. In addition to leis, the locals are known throughout Polynesia for their hand woven pandanus mats and bowls. Electrical service on Mauke is full time, or at least it is intended that way, occasional outages will occur, primarily in severe weather.

Getting There

The majority of visitors fly from Rarotonga on **Air Rarotonga Ph. 35-888** (Mauke) **Ph. 22-888** (Rarotonga); there are three weekly flights on Monday, Wednesday and Friday. If you are planning on visiting other islands in the southern group you will want to purchase a multi island package, as this will result in a cost savings. See the **Getting Around** section in the front of this book for information. Island freighters do make trips to Mauke from Rarotonga. You will want to read the section in the front of this book referring to Inter-Island freighters before considering this method of travel.

Getting Around

There is no public transportation on Mauke, so the only alternative is to walk. Your guesthouse may have motorbikes and bicycles that you can rent for sightseeing at your own pace. Hitchhiking is frowned upon, and frankly, you may not see a vehicle headed your way for a couple of hours, so as I said walking is the alternative. Be sure and wear sturdy shoes, for if you are walking on the local coral or *makatea* strong shoes are a must.

Things To Do

How about a divided church for a starter? Due to an age-old dispute between the two villages of Ngatiarua and Areora, the church was divided in the center and each village decorated their own side. The dividers were long ago removed, but a trip to the Zion Church reveals the dual gateways that lead to the twin entry doors of Mauke's largest church. The church itself is one of the most unique buildings in the Cook Islands; check out the interlocking arches and the colorful designs within the building.

Caves, caves and more caves. The Vai Tonga Cave is a ten-minute walk from Ngatiarua Village and therefore the easiest to access from either the Mauke Cove Lodge or Tiare Cottages. The cave is one of several on the island and features a clear fresh water pool. The Motuanga Cave is located on the southern part of the island and I suggest enlisting the help of a guide if you want to explore the "cave of a hundred rooms." The entrance is through a narrow hole in the *makatea.* Once you are inside you crawl through two caves to the third, which contains a large deep-water pool. Wear sturdy shoes for walking on the sharp coral and take along a flashlight for it is dark in the cave.

The island is small, only 12 miles in circumference, so a walk around the entire island takes only about three hours. The south and east sides of the island are uninhabited, so the beaches in these areas are quite secluded. As I have stated numerous times in this book. A slow walk around the island will serve as an invitation to the curious children, they will want to know who you are, where you are from and how long you will be on their island. Their parents will have more questions for you and hopefully you will have questions of them. Soon, you will be meeting the town elders and finding out who is going fishing and when, and before you know it, you will be coming over for dinner and playing cards on Saturday. If you stay long enough you will forget you are a tourist and leave the rest of the world behind. I just can't over stress the friendliness of the islanders, so forgive the fact that I repeat this paragraph almost word for word when describing all outer islands in the Cook Island chain.

Friday is market day and a chance to purchase the local handicrafts. Look for hand woven *pandanus* mats, baskets, purses and hats with bright borders and mother of pearl inlays. The island men carve attractive wooden bowls and miniature canoes. If you are not in the buying mood, just mingle with the locals and sample the various food items for sale at the market.

The market place is a good source of local fruit and as always a chance to experience local culture and meet islanders.

There is little nightlife on Mauke, or at least as we know it. The islands only full time bar is **Tura's Ph. 35-023,** which is located off the main road, near the college. The bar is open on a very limited basis, usually only on Friday nights. A second bar on the island **Toianga's** is open on Friday and Saturday nights, if you have your own booze you can take it to Toianga's, they don't mind. Ask around for directions to either bar. Saturday night is bingo night at the Catholic Church. You can enquire at your accommodation to see if one of the occasional dances is scheduled while you are on the island.

If you are on the island over a Sunday, be sure and visit the CICC church to experience the singing and worship services. While hardly a religious person myself, a visit to any Cook Island church service is a wonderful and spiritual experience, that never fails to bring tears to my eyes.

Places To Stay

Outer island accommodations are typically quite basic. Expect a basic room with hopefully a fan and lights. Showers are basic; some lodgings have heated showers, while others are served by catchment water, which is usually quite pleasant if not refreshing. Short showers are the rule, as water supplies are limited. Try and book you're lodging at least a week in advance, food supplies are limited and depending on when the last inter-island ship stopped at the island food may e in short supply. Ask if you can bring anything with you from Rarotonga, especially if you desire a steak or hamburger. Mauke will have plenty of local fish, pork and island grown fruits and vegetables, take advantage of the local items as they are as freshest you will ever find.

Tiare Holiday Cottages, Ph. 35-083, Fax 35-683
P.O. Box 75, Mauke Island, Cook Islands
Website: www.mauke.com
E-Mail: te4ta@mauke.net.ck

Long the staple in Mauke, Tiare Holiday Cottages are moving into their second generation as an accommodation. Original hosts Tautuara and Kura Purea are retiring and their daughter and son-in-law Teata and Tangata Ateriano have taken over the reigns at this famous lodging.

Step one in the change over was the hand made *O'Kiva* cottage that Tangata built on the *makatea* cliffs overlooking the reef. The cottage is a short walk away from the main area, up a gravel path through a thicket. There is a small covered patio on the front and once inside you will be impressed with Tangata's amazing construction skills. The unit has a custom tile shower in a modern stylish bathroom. The studio features a queen sized bed, table and chairs, refrigerator and microwave. Walls are native woods with shell and coral accents to remind you of where you that you are on an island. Not that you would forget, with the gentle sound of the waves on the reef providing constant background music. The highlight of *O'Kiva* is up a path behind the cottage, which leads to a covered viewing platform. The memory of the sunset view from this platform, will remind you for a lifetime of the time you spent on Mauke.

The second individual cottage is known as *Rupe,* with a private garden setting through the trees to a view of the ocean. This cottage features a single bed as well as a queen sized bed and can be converted to a family unit to sleep up to four people. Completing the holiday cottages are two semi-detached studios which both offer a single and double bed, indoor bath and light tea and coffee making facilities.

Meals at Tiare are served family style in a covered outdoor eating area and kitchen. If you are planning on eating your meals at Tiare, notify the owners so that they can arrange for food prior to your arrival.

These island style bungalows are located in the village of Kimiangatau, near the ocean and close to the airport. The owners will be happy to assist you with tours or fishing. Scooter rental is available at Tiare, rates are NZ$25.00 per day. The studio rates are NZ$70.00/$75.00 for single/double with the family cottage (Rupe) NZ$75.00/$85.00 for single/double. The honeymoon lodge (O'Kiva) rents for NZ$135.00 for single or double.

Ri's Hideaway, Ph. (682) 35-181
Anaraura Beach, Mauke Island, <u>Cook Islands</u>
E-Mail: <u>ris-retreat@mauke.net.ck</u>

There are five individual cottages on stilts over on Anaraura Beach, which certainly qualify as a hideaway, as they are all by themselves with nothing else within a couple of miles. You will want to make sure that you arrange for a scooter if you are staying at the hideaway. The units all have ocean views, though the units are away from the beach a bit. Each has a covered patio with with table and chairs. The five are on a rather small plot and thus fairly close together. Each is fully self-contained and equipped with fans. Rates are NZ$85.00/$115.00 for single/double per night.

Ri's Retreat, Ph. (682) 35-181
Airport Road, Mauke Island, <u>Cook Islands</u>
E-Mail: <u>ris-retreat@mauke.net.ck</u>

These three units are near the airport are the older of Ri's "hotel empire" on Mauke. They feature small covered patios and have ensuite bathrooms. Though somewhat older they are brightly decorated and offer reasonable value for the price. If it was up to me I prefer the hideaway units to the airport units. Rates for the units at the Retreat are NZ$85.00/$115.00 for single/double.

Places To Eat

If you are staying at Tiare Holiday Cottages meals can be provided. If you are staying at Ri's you will need to prepare your own meals or arrange with Tiare to come by for some of your meals. If you brought along some food and hopefully you did, you can prepare your own meals at all but the O'Kiva cottage at Tiare, which has no kitchen. In lieu of that there are five small convenience stores on the island; four of those are in the inland villages of Ngatiarua and Areora. Just ask around for **Tua Traders, Kato's, Ariki's** and **Virginia's Store**. The fifth is over in the coastal village of Kimiangatau and it is known as **Mauke Trading**. The inland village also has the islands only bakery, just ask around for **Willy's Bakery**, anyone will be able to point you to Willy, as with all bakers, arrive early to insure that bread is available. You can pick up locally grown produce at the Mauke market, which is only open on Friday's; the market is located near the wharf, shop early for the best selection.

Mitiaro

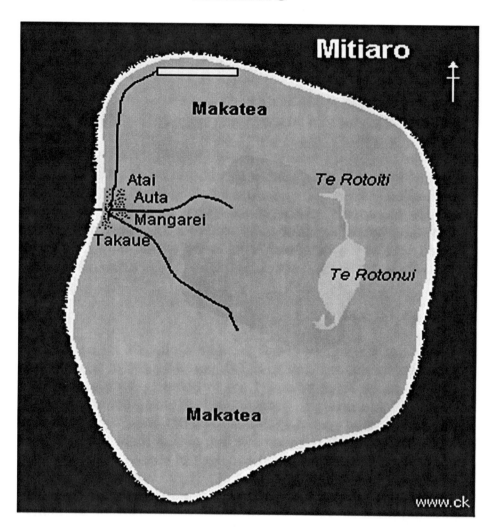

A trip to any of the smaller outlying Cook Islands is a treat that is difficult to duplicate. While Mitiaro is the fourth largest of the Cook Islands in landmass, there are less than 200 inhabitants on this relatively flat island. My trip in March of 2008 coincided with a birthday celebration for one of the construction workers on the islands elementary school. The party was at the home of my host and I was immediately instructed that I was to be a special guest. The party included a feast with local flying fish as well as prodigious amounts of New Zealand beer and a few bottles of Jim Beam. The merriment went on well past my bedtime, with the hostess chasing away stragglers at 4:00 AM. During the night I was toasted by the Island Minister and the Mayor of the village, the birthday boy, was a skinny Puka Pukan who was to become forty-two the next day. The sound of traditional island songs, sung by my newfound brothers, echoed from under the coconut palms. The music was wonderful and the memories of that night will last a lifetime, the hangover was gone by noon, but the boys were back and ready to start over again by breakfast.

Mitiaro Island is the fourth largest Island in the Cook Islands chain and lies approximately 140 miles Northeast of Rarotonga. The island is of volcanic origin and is surrounded by a belt of fossilized coral or makatea that is also a major feature on it's fellow southern group island Mangaia. Mitiaro is only about thirty miles from its nearest neighbor in the southern group Atiu. Historically, the people of Atiu would sail over to Mitiaro when they were low on food or in search of wives. The soil on Mitiaro was superior to the soil on Atiu thus they had a larger variety of crops. It is undocumented if the soil produced superior women, but faced with slim prospects at home, the Atiuan warriors returned with a bride or two. The current population of the island is around two hundred, so you quickly become part of the island's extended family when you visit. Visit Mitiaro to enjoy a quiet paced, eco-friendly trip to a land with natural beauty and kind friendly islanders, in a totally non-commercial type South Sea Island environment. In recent years electric service has been expanded to full time service, in the past electricity was a part time occurrence, as you can see progress is coming to the outer islands.

Getting There

Visitors to Mitiaro fly direct from Rarotonga on **Air Rarotonga Ph. 36-888** (Mitiaro) **Ph. 22-888** (Rarotonga); there are two weekly flights, on Monday and Friday. If you are planning on visiting other islands in the southern group you will want to purchase a multi-island package, as this will result in a cost savings. See the **Getting Around** section in the front of this book for information. Island freighters do make trips to Mitiaro from Rarotonga, please read the section in the front of this book referring to Inter-Island freighters before considering this method of travel.

Getting Around

There is no public transportation on Mitiaro, so the only alternative is to walk. Your guesthouse will meet you at the airport and may have motorbikes and bicycles that you can rent for sightseeing at your own pace. Hitchhiking is frowned upon, and frankly, you may not see a vehicle headed your way for a couple of hours, so as I said walking is the alternative. Be sure and wear sturdy shoes, for if you are walking on the local coral or *makatea,* strong shoes are a must.

Things To Do

A major feature on Mitiaro is the two fresh water lakes, both of which contain indigenous eels or, *itiki,* which are regarded as a delicacy in the Cook Islands. It is easy to arrange a guided visit to the lakes or a fishing trip with a local guide. Enquire at your accommodation. If you are lodging and they will put you in touch with a local fisherman. If you are going to visit the lakes, be sure and bring along some insect repellant to ward of any mosquitoes.

Tours of the island can be arranged by contacting **Papa Neke Ph. 36-347.** Chances are he will take you by his island retreat as well as showing you the various island highlights.

The many limestone caves on the island provide a great opportunity for swimming. You can arrange a trip to the Vai Nature Cave for a swim. Most of the locals swim at the caves and are only too happy to take a visitor along. If you prefer, ask at your guesthouse for a guide to take you to a *maka* for a swim

The fortress at *Te Pare* was where the original inhabitants of Mitiaro hid when those pesky Aituans came over in search of food and women. This practice has long since been discontinued, but a visit to the fortress is worthwhile, ask for directions at your guesthouse. On occasion, the local tourism officer **Julian Aupuni Ph. 36-180** will lead tours of the fort, you can call him up and ask how busy his schedule is during your visit.

The island is only 11 miles in circumference, so a walk around the entire island takes only about three hours. If you are on the island over a Sunday, be sure and visit the white painted CICC church to experience the singing and worship services. If you go for a walk, leave yourself plenty of time to visit with the locals; the pace on the island is such that everyone has time to talk. Children on the island will be curious as to where you are from and how long you will be on the island, their parents will have more questions for you and hopefully you will have questions of them. Soon, you will be meeting the town elders and finding out who is going fishing and when, and before you know it, you will be coming over for dinner and playing cards on Saturday. If you stay long enough you will forget you are a tourist and leave the rest of the world behind

Places To Stay

Outer island accommodations are typically quite basic. Expect a basic room with hopefully a fan and lights. Showers on Mitiaro are all basic, at the time this is written, no lodging has heated showers, but are served by catchment water, which is usually quite pleasant if not refreshing. Short showers are the rule, as water supplies are limited. Try and book you're lodging at least a week in advance, food supplies are limited and depending on when the last inter-island ship stopped at the island food may be in short supply. Ask if you can bring anything with you from Rarotonga, especially if you desire a steak or hamburger. Mitiaro will have plenty of local fish, pork and island grown fruits and vegetables, take advantage of the local items, as they are as fresh as you will ever find.

Seabreeze Lodge, Phone 36-153, Fax 36-165
Website: www.jetsave.co.ck/mitiaro_island.htm
Mitiaro Island, Cook Islands
E-mail: jetsave@cooks.co.ck

At the time this is written, Jane Herman, the original owners daughter and proprietor of Seabreeze Lodge is off in Australia and the Lodge is closed. Reliable sources tell me that it is likely that the Lodge will re-open this summer (2008). If that is not the case, there may not be any tourist accommodations on Mitiaro, which would really be a shame. The Tourist Board informed the author that they could not help with my lodging on Mitiaro, as

they had no accredited facility on the island. Don't ask me to go into how I feel about a tourism board that will not at least give you some names of people who live on Mitiaro. Silly me, I thought it should be their job to assist all tourists.

Hopefully Seabreeze will be up and running soon. If so, you can call and book direct with Jane Herman or book with Jetsave Travel for the self contained two-bedroom unit with private bathroom facilities, or the two bedrooms in the main building. Prices include all meals, but if you book direct you can elect to bring your food with you and prepare your own meals. Ms. Herman is known for her excellent cooking and a stay at Seabreeze will allow you to experience true Mitiaro hospitality. The last rates quoted NZ$75.00 per person and you can add a child for NZ$44.00. The shower is at room temperature and not heated.

Nukuroa Beach Guesthouse Phone 36-106
Mitiaro Island, Cook Islands
Website: www.jetsave.co.ck/mitiaro_island.htm
E-mail: jetsave@cooks.co.ck

Stay at the Nukuroa Beach Guesthouse and you will be staying with the un-official queen of Mitiaro. The 'queen' will rent you a motorbike, prepare all your meals and assist you with island tours to ensure that your trip to Mitiaro is an enjoyable experience. This is a home-stay type accommodation, so your toilet facilities are shared. As it is with all lodgings on Mitiaro, showers are at room temperature, not cold but not heated. Actually the showers are quite refreshing once you grow accustomed to the idea. Rates are NZ$82.00 for single/twin or triple, including three meals per day. A child can be added for $44.00 per day. In recent years two new rooms were added at Nukuroa.

Ngatoa Lodge, Ph. (682) 36-003
Mitiaro Island, <u>Cook Islands</u>
E-Mail: <u>vivian@oyster.net.ck</u>

Vivian Vandongen has two rooms in her combination convenience store/home in Takaue Village. On the same property is a separate private studio unit. The studio has a nice

 view of the ocean through the trees. The two bedrooms in the main house are small, bright and clean, there is a shared bath with unheated shower. All meals are provided by the owner and included in the following rates. The studio unit rents for NZ$125.00/$165.00 for single/double and the two rooms in the main house are

NZ$75.00/$95.00 for single/double. Vivian will assist on tour plans and scooter rental for guests. Access to a small beach is a short walk from the lodge. Airport transfers are NZ$5.00 per person.

Places To Eat

You will be eating all three of your meals at the guesthouse where you are staying, but there is a small shop or two on the island where you can purchase some snacks. Go by **Patai Store Ph. 36-003** or **Pa's Store Ph. 36-155**, both of which are located in Takaue Village near the CICC Church, just ask anyone for directions. You will want to bring along some of your favorite packaged snacks to Mitiaro, as the shops have only basic items

Penrhyn

It was dawn as the Manu Nui began its journey through the Taruia Passage into Penrhyn's huge lagoon. We had spent the night anchored off the island, fishing and watching the sparkling lights that outlined the Catholic Church on the Northern edge of the village of Omoka. The dock at Omoka was our intended destination when and if we made it through the passage into the lagoon. The tide was receding as our ship entered the passage. We would surge forward with each new wave, only to be pulled back as the tide overcame the force of the wave. On both sides of the ship waves crashed on the reef with a giant roar as we steamed ahead intent upon reaching the dock in Omoka. In time it was apparent that we were making headway, we were slowly gaining on the tide. In the middle of the ship's struggle the sun rose and a rainbow was visible within the spray of the breaking surf. It was as if the sunrise marked our victory over the conditions. Within seconds we reached the safety of the lagoon and minutes later the dock at Omoka. Just the start of another day in the South Pacific for the islanders, but the memory of a lifetime for an American writer far from his It home.

Penrhyn is the northernmost Island of the Cook Islands chain. It is 850 miles from Rarotonga, 220 miles north of Manihiki and sees few tourists. It is one of the largest atolls in the South Pacific and its huge lagoon constitutes one of the few safe harbors in this region of the South Seas. There are around 500 residents on this island and they exist as sustenance farmers and fisherman. There is pearl farming taking place in the lagoon at Penrhyn, but it is of a smaller scale than the pearl farming done on Manihiki. The population of Penrhyn is primarily distributed between the commercial village of Omoka and the more agricultural village of Te Tautua, which is located on the

more fertile Pokerekere. Te Tautua has about half the population of Omoka, but produces the majority of the fruit crops of paw paw (papaya), Kuru (breadfruit) and bananas.

Getting There

The few visitors that do visit Penrhyn fly from Rarotonga on Air Rarotonga Ph. 42-888 (Penrhyn) Ph. 22-888 (Rarotonga); there is but one weekly flight on Saturday. If you are planning on visiting other islands you will want to purchase a multi island package, as this will result in a cost savings. See the Getting Around section in the front of this book for information. Island freighters do make occasional trips to Penrhyn from Rarotonga, please read the section in the front of this book referring to Inter-Island freighters before considering this method of travel.

Getting Around

There is no public transportation on Penrhyn, so the only alternative is to walk. Hitchhiking is frowned upon, and frankly, you may not see a vehicle headed your way for a couple of hours. As I said walking is the alternative.

Things To Do

You will be most likely staying in Omoka if you are visiting Penrhyn, as both the boat dock and airstrip are located in this main village. Omoka is located on the island of Moananui on the west side of the lagoon. The island is quite small, so a walk around the entire island takes only a couple of hours. If you are on the island over a Sunday, be sure and visit the white painted CICC church to experience the singing and worship services. If you go for a walk, leave yourself plenty of time to visit with the locals; the pace on the island is such that everyone has time to talk. Children on the island will be curious as to where you are from and how long you will be on the island. Their parents will have more questions for you and hopefully you will have questions of them. Soon, you will be meeting the town elders and finding out who is going fishing and when, and before you know it, you will be coming over for dinner and playing cards on Saturday. If you stay long enough you will forget you are a tourist and leave the rest of the world behind.

A stay on any of the islands in the Northern Cook's is an activity the likes of which you will probably never encounter in your life. Savor it and experience a simple life in this unique environment. For a short time, enjoy island life surrounded by a lagoon that is truly one of the earth's natural wonders. Besides, think of all the stories you will have to tell when you return stateside.

Places To Stay

Soa's Guesthouse, Ph. 42-018, Fax. 42-105
Omoka Village, Penrhyn Island, <u>Cook Islands</u>

This guesthouse is located in a three-bedroom home in the main village of Omoka. Host Soatini will prepare three meals a day, take you fishing and show you his pearl farm. Showers are typical out island, meaning the water is not heated. The electrical power on Penrhyn is also typical out island, meaning the electricity goes off about midnight and does not come on again until around 5:00 AM. Take along a flashlight if you have a weak bladder for the trip to the communal toilet facilities. Rates are listed as NZ$82.00 per day single or double. Bookings are made through Jetsave Travel in Rarotonga, Ph. 27-707, fax 27-807 or visit the Website and or E-mail to the sites shown above.

Terakora Guesthouse, Ph. 42-019, Fax. 42-863
Omoka Village, Penrhyn Island, <u>Cook Islands</u>

Terakora Guesthouse is located in a local home and like Soa's; the hosts Puria & Doreen Heria will provide all meals in a family setting. Rates are NZ$85.00 per person and I would suggest booking in advance.

Tongareva Sunrise Units, Ph. &B Fax 42-027
Amoka Village, Penrhyn Island, <u>Cook Islands</u> Website:
<u>www.jetsave.co.ck/penrhyn island.htm</u>
E-mail: <u>jetsave@cooks.co.ck</u>

This 2-bedroom self-catering unit is located on the lagoon between the airport and Amoka Village. Each of the two bedrooms has a double and single bed and ceiling fans. Each bedroom has a separate bathroom with flush toilet and shower. The shared kitchen features a refrigerator, range, oven toaster and coffee service. There is a nearby mini-mart with limited supplies. All towels, linens and bedding supplied. Owners can arrange scooter rental, fishing, island tours and visits to a pearl farm. Electricity on Penrhyn is on 6:00 AM to 11:00 PM daily. Your hosts the Tonittara family will insure that your visit to Penrhyn is an enjoyable experience. Rates for the rooms are NZ$75.00 per night single/double, bookings can be made direct or through Jetsave Travel in Rarotonga

There are no other organized accommodations presently on Penrhyn. The only other accommodations would have to be a home stay. Talk to the tourist board in Avarua before you leave Rarotonga. They may have some names or you can talk to the various pastors of churches if you arrive on Penrhyn without accommodation, nobody will stay homeless long with the generosity of these islanders, but keep in mind there limited resources.

Places To Eat

As there are no restaurants on Penrhyn, you will likely be eating all three of your meals at the guesthouse where you are staying.

There are some small shops on the island where you can purchase some snacks, but supplies are limited and selection will be dependent on how close you are to a freighter visit during your stay. You will want to bring along some of your favorite packaged snacks to Penrhyn, as the shops have only basic items.

Atiu

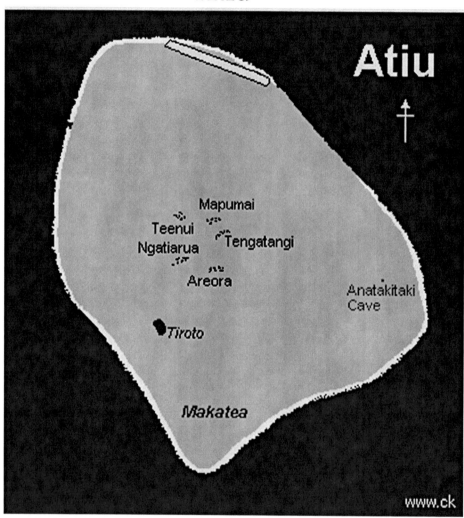

When I first visited Atiu in 2003, there were a variety of changes taking place on the island. Kia Orana Bungalows was under construction and Atiu Villas was completing their fifth and sixth villas. Now that may not sound like much, but the island was increasing its tourist bed count by nearly forty percent. There was a newly formed tourism board and sleepy little Atiu was becoming discovered.

In ensuing five years, there has been little further growth. Atiu Villas put in a swimming pool and Terangi-Nui Café opened its doors in Areora. So I was surprised when I started hearing rumors about several proposals for large-scale resorts with golf courses and spas. Well let's hope that talk of large-scale development, remains in the rumor and talking phase for a very long time. I know local Autuans and this author would like to see the island remain the unspoiled queen of the Cook Islands.

Atiu's traditional island name is, *Enua Manu*, which translates to 'land of the birds' and there are several varieties on the island, some of which are exclusive to Atiu. In recent years several pairs of Rarotongan Flycatchers were transplanted to Atiu, after they became nearly extinct on their home island. It seems they were the favorite meal of rats that came to Rarotonga on ships from other ports. Since Atiu has no harbor, rats had not migrated to the island and thus the flycatcher was safe. Since the move the small bird has made a great comeback and can be heard and seen in the trees on the road to the airport. The rats are quite unhappy and can be seen back in Rarotonga, sorting through the trash at the Waterfront Café in Avarua.

If you are a birdwatcher you may want to keep an eye open for the *kopeka*, the local name for the Atiu Swiftlet. It is said that the Tahiti Swiflet and the Atiu version are nearly identical and can only be told apart by holding one in each hand. It is not known how you are to possibly accomplish this task, for smuggling birds into French Polynesia is probably a capital offense, but you know those birdwatchers are a strange sort. Birdwatchers tell me the swiflet never lands except to lay its eggs. It is unclear if the male swiflet ever lands and frankly I'd like to know if those wacky birdwatchers work in shifts and if not how do they know they never land? They may just wait for the birdwatchers to fall asleep and then take a major rest break. Please send the study results to the address in the front of the book and I will apologize to birdwatchers worldwide in the next edition of the book; but for now I am not buying it.

The main village on Atiu, Areora is located in the center of the volcanic island. One of the main features of Atiu is the cliffs of fossilized coral, or *makatea,* as it is known in Maori. It forms a ring around the perimeter of Atiu and is in common with most islands that make up the southern group. By whatever name you call it, the first time you try to walk on *makatea*, you will understand why the islanders built their village in the center of the island. The good news is if you skirt the *makatea* and get down to the beach you will be rewarded by finding your own private beach. The lagoon is narrow and the reef in close proximity of the beach, but you can splash around and acquire a tan all by yourself. Who cares about those little birds?

My favorite coral, *makatea* has also created a labyrinth of caves on Atiu, you will need to hire a guide as the caves are on private land. Pesky little kopeka birds inhabit one cave in particular, Anatakitaki Cave. I am not making this up, they really are in the cave, trust me I saw them. Of course I had been at the native bush beer school, locally known as the *Tumunu* the night before and it was pretty dark in the cave. Well it was dark in George's Datsun pick up truck and I never really went **into** the cave, but George said he saw the *kopekas* and after all he is the guide!

Getting There

The vast majority of visitors fly from Rarotonga on **Air Rarotonga Ph. 33-888** (Atiu) **Ph. 22-888** (Rarotonga); there are daily flights to Atiu, the Tuesday and Wednesday flights connect through Mauke and Mitiaro respectfully. If you are planning on visiting other islands in the southern group you will want to purchase a multi island package, as this will result in a cost savings. See the **Getting Around** section in the front of this book for information. Island freighters do make trips to Atiu from Rarotonga, please read the section in the front of this book referring to Inter-Island freighters before considering this method of travel.

Getting Around

All accommodations on the island can arrange for or provide rental scooters or bicycles. Costs vary but you can figure to pay around NZ$25.00 a day for a scooter and NZ$10.00 a day for a mountain bike. Try **T&J Rentals Ph. 33-271** in the village of Tengatangi, near the new traffic circle, they rent bikes and scooters. If you wish to rent a car or truck, let your accommodation know ahead of time so that they can try to arrange a rental, as there are few rental cars and trucks on the island. The cost will be around NZ$60.00 per day. There is no public transportation on Atiu, so the only alternative is to hoof it. Hitchhiking is frowned upon, so as I said, walking is the alternative.

Things to Do

There are more things to do on Atiu than the much more visited Aitutaki. Atiu has caves, nature and birding tours, a couple of coffee plantation tours, a historical tour and a fiber arts factory as well as many secluded beaches to discover on your rental scooter. On Atiu you can go fishing with locals either offshore on a boat or off the reef.

So take your pick, contact George Mateariki, better known as "Birdman George" of **George's Nature Walk Ph. 33-047** for a nature or bird watching tour, the tour lasts three hours and costs

NZ$30.00. George can show you the Rarotongan flycatcher that was near extinction a few years ago until being moved to Atiu. The tour is also known as a mosquitoes feeding tour as George leads you into the brush off the airport road to a nest and hopefully a sighting of the rare bird. The day I went we spotted an adult gray flycatcher while feeding the mosquitoes, I'm just kidding, George. The "Birdman" will call the birds and they will fly to George and his tour guests. At the completion of the tour a light lunch is served. Marshall Humphrey's' over at **Atiu Tours Ph. 33-041** or e-mail **marshall@atiutours.co.ck** leads island tours at a cost of NZ$40.00 for adults, children 5-12 NZ$15.00 and under 5 free of charge, as well as caving tours for NZ$20.00 for adults and NZ$10.00 for children ages 5-12. Those taking tours and staying at the Humphrey's Accommodation receive a 10% discount on their tour cost. For a tour of the **Atiu Coffee Plantation Ph. 33-030** or e-mail **coffee@adc,co.ck** the cost of the coffee factory tour is NZ$15.00 each, with a minimum of two people on the tour. Jurgen Manske-Eimke, the German born coffee maker arrived on Atiu in the 1980's and constructed his small factory on Atiu and has been making his gourmet coffee ever since. In recent years a second coffee tour has been added. **Mata Aria Ph. 33-088** is a descendent of a family that grew coffee in Atiu back in the fifties and she returned about ten years ago to Atiu and her wild coffee fields. Mata's coffee is still handpicked, sun dried and hand roasted the old fashioned way. While neither Peets nor Starbuck's have tendered any offers, both Atiu coffee makers, have avid followers and offer samples as part of their tours. Mata's tour cost is NZ$15.00, the same price as Atiu Coffee Plantation, both tours offer coffee at discount prices at the end of the tour.

If you would like to try your hand at reef fishing call up **Papa Moetaua Ph. 33-013** and have him take you fishing on the reef. Papa will furnish the pole, but tours depend on the water and tides. The cost of the tour is NZ$25.00 each. If you would like to learn more about Atiu's history and culture, be sure and take **Papa Paiere's Ph. 33-034** interesting and informative historical tour. Paiere Mokoroa is one of Atiu's last living storytellers, a retired teacher at Atiu College and a fountain of knowledge about the history of the island.

To try your hand at deep-sea fishing or admire Atiu from the perspective of the sea, call **Tokoa Kea Ph. 33-040.** He offers sightseeing trips for NZ$50.00 and fishing trips for NZ$60.00 per person on his 28' aluminum boat with a 90 horsepower outboard. The three-hour fishing trips take a maximum of three passengers, while on the two-hour sightseeing trips he can take up to five passengers. The boat is also available for charters so call TK, as he is known on the island, and schedule a voyage.

No visit to Atiu is complete without a visit to a *Tumunu*, or bush beer school as they are sometimes called. I have to admit that my dinner host Roger Malcomb, proprietor of the Atiu Villas lured me down the evil path to the school. Not only was I taken to a Tumunu, but I was taken to the twice champion *Tamariki Te Donui Tumunu,* which roughly translates into the **'Big Night Boys Tumunu' Ph. 33-443** which it truly was. We had a great old time me and the big night boys, passing around the cup of tropical white lightning, which it turns out does not taste bad, and in fact tastes better than some home brew I have tasted in the states. But more about the Tumunu and why the big night boys are champions. It seems for the past couple of years they have designated visitors to the various Tumunu to serve as honorary judges and these judges after careful consideration and consumption of copious amounts of joy juice has determined the Big Night Boys, the champions. Believe it or not the Big Night Boys have a phone at the Tumunu and you can call them up and see what's happening at the Tumunu. Ask for Apii, the rubanesque treasurer of the group, he loves to show off the lights, ceiling fan and flushing toilet that are all part of the award winning Tumunu. I am currently negotiating a franchise for California, so be sure and tell him Papa Mike sent you. They have not screened off the neighboring mosquitoes, so be sure and bring along some repellant and NZ$5.00 for the ingredients for the next batch of bush beer.

Places To Stay

Are Manuiri Guesthouse, Ph. 33-031, Fax. 33-032
P.O. Box 13, Atiu, <u>Cook Islands</u>
Website: <u>www.adc.co.ck</u>
E-mail: <u>adc@adc.co.ck</u>

Located in Areora village, the guesthouse has three bedrooms, one family sized (queen and single) and two with twin beds. Shower and bathroom facilities are shared, as is the kitchen and dining room. There is a thatched roof verandah at the front of

the house, which receives a nice cool breeze on most days and is an excellent spot to watch village life or enjoy a cup of fresh Atiu coffee direct from owner Jurgen Eimke's local coffee plantation. Rates at the guesthouse are NZ$30.00 for a single bed in shared room, NZ$60.00 for a single bed in a room to yourself and $75.00 for the family room. Children under 12 are not permitted at Are Manuiri. To the rates above add NZ$14.00 each way for airport transfers. Tours and rental bikes and scooters can be arranged and the Eimke's have a Daihatsu jeep that you can rent for NZ$65.00. The neighbor children are the un-official greeters at Are Manuiri and they will pop over to chat and find out where you are from. The guesthouse is spacious and cozy and I loved the verandah.

Atiu Villas, Ph. 33-777, Fax. 33-775
P.O. Box 7, Atiu, Cook Islands
Website: www.atiu.info/atiuvillas
E-mail: atiu@ihug.co.nz

Roger and Kura Malcolm's Atiu Villas is past the village of  Areora on the road to Matai landing. There are currently five self-contained one-bedroom units that sleep up to three people and one family unit that will sleep up to four people. The six units are of A-frame type construction, and were the first visitor accommodations, operating continuously since the early 1980's. The owners have put a lot of hard work into the villas and associated buildings and the finished property, complete with last year's swimming pool addition is proof that hard work and diligence eventually pays off. The villas come fully stocked with groceries when you arrive, and you pay only for what you use, which on a small island is not only convenient, but takes away the nuisance of having to find a store and shop for goods. There is an open-air thatch roof restaurant on premises for visitors and guests, which is open for evening meals. Rates at the villas are NZ$110.00/ NZ$120.00 for single/double. Island night festivities are available at Atiu Villas, the local dance group will show up and perform for NZ$100, the cost of which can be split between the Villa guests and any outsiders wishing to attend. Celebrating your anniversary, hire the dance troupe for the night and have them all to yourself.

Taparere Lodge, Ph. 33-034, Fax 33-034
Atiu, Cook Islands
E-mail: mac@oyster.net.ck

There are two self-contained studio units at Nga & Paiere Mokaroa's lodge, located on the edge of the main village of Teenui; down a side road. Under construction is a third self-contained studio unit as well as a fourth unit that is in the process of being converted into a backpacker unit with multiple beds. Rates have not been established on the backpacker beds, but will be competitive with like units in Rarotonga and Aitutaki. All the units overlook a pine forest, plantations and native fern lands. All units except the backpacker unit, has two double beds and a single bed, rates are NZ$65.00 single in shared rooms, twins and doubles are NZ$78.00, with a per person extra rate of NZ$20.00. All units have mosquito netting and are cooled by fans. Let Nga know ahead of time if you don't want to share a room. Papa Paiere conducts historical tours of the island, see what to do section in this chapter.

Kopeka Lodge, Ph. 33-283, Fax. 33-284
P.O. Box 746, Atiu, Cook Islands
E-mail: stay@kopekalodge-atiu.co.ck

The three-unit Kopeka Lodge is located on the outskirts of Areora Village on the road to Takauroa beach. Kopeka Lodge has one studio bungalow and a couple of two-bedroom bungalows. The self-contained clapboard units have large wooden decks and are located in a quiet peaceful neighborhood. The lodging's name, "Kopeka" is derived from Atiu's rare bird according to Kopeka's owner/operator Mann Unuia. Rates at Kopeka Lodge are NZ$85.00/NZ$95.00/NZ$105.00 for single/double/triple. Four adults in the same lodge will pay NZ$125.00. Mann tells me he has flexible rates for children traveling with parents and will offer discounts for extended stays. All lodges are fully screened, have hot and cold water and feature pedestal fans. Airport transfers are NZ$15.00 each way, children under 12 are half price. Seasonal rates are currently under consideration but as of yet not finalized, check with Mann by E-mail to find out if any changes to rates have been finalized.

Kia Orana Bungalows, Ph./Fax (682) 33-013
PO Box 9, Atiu, <u>Cook Islands</u>
Website: <u>www.atiutourism.com/kia_orana_bungalows.htm</u>
E-Mail: <u>boaza@kia_orana.co.ck</u>

As I awaited my flight at the tiny airport on Atiu, I was introduced to Papa Moetaua the owner of the newest, and at that time unnamed accommodation on the island. We discussed names and he liked the name Kia Orana. I see that the name stuck and his six wooden self-contained bungalows are now in full operation. Located on the outskirts of Areora Village not far from Atiu Villas, there are three bungalows with double beds and three with twin single beds. Each bungalow has a private verandah with table, chairs and a view of Atiu's rainforest. Rates are NZ$80.00 for single/double and airport transfers are an additional NZ$15.00 per person. Papa Motaua, patriarch of the Boaza Clan, which operates Kia Orana, can usually be found supervising operations. Talk to Papa about renting one of his scooters, when he is not busy supervising construction of the restaurant, he leads reef fishing tours at a nominal rate.

**Atiu Homestay (B&B), Ph. 33-041,
PO Box 14, Atiu, <u>Cook Islands</u>
Website: <u>www.atiutoursaccommodation.com</u>
E-Mail: <u>marshall@atiutours.co.ck</u>**

Marshall and Jeanne Humphreys have been running island and cave tours on Atiu for a number of years. Jeanne is the daughter of the famous Tom Neale, who is a noted Cook Islands author and better known as the hermit of Suwarrow. Marshall is from mother England and has an extensive background in the hotel and travel industry. Their four bedroom home offers one bedroom with twin beds, and two double rooms with a double and queen sized bed. The house is located in a rural setting outside of the village with a verandah overlooking extensive gardens. Rates include a tropical breakfast and additional meals can be arranged. Guests receive a ten percent discount on island and cave tours conducted by Marshall. Scooter and vehicle hire can be arranged, subject to availability. Rates are NZ$40.00 per person, children under 13 years of age are not permitted. Return airport transfers are NZ$20.00 per person.

Where To Eat

The good news is **Kura's Kitchen Ph. 33-777** at Aitu Villas, serves excellent dinners; the bad news is it is the only restaurant on the island and only open evenings. The night I was there Bella, the villa's new cook and assistant to Kura, wife of Roger Malcolm the quick-witted owner of Atiu Villas, served us an excellent spaghetti bolognaise. Roger that night was intent upon finding a proper suitor for Bella, while Kura was bemoaning the potential loss of her newfound cook and having to return to the kitchen. Keep in mind that the dinner was after our trip to the *Tumunu*, so we were feeling no pain and myself and the two male guests from Austria proclaimed that Bella should stay on as cook and with that we had another round of beers before they turned in and I hopped on my scooter to return to Are Manuiri. As far as I know Bella is still cooking and if my memory serves me well the dinner and three beers was around NZ$30.00.

While Atiu is still awaiting it's first Starbucks, it does appear that a second restaurant has opened on the island. **Terangi Nui Café Ph. 33-101** serves tropical breakfast, light lunches and full dinners from their location in the village of Areora. Atuian Parua Tavioni has returned after a stint in the catering business in Kiwi land and has returned to offer some competition to Kura Malcolm over at Atiu Villas. No news as to when the cook off will occur, but the recent increase in tourist arrivals indicates that additional food options are much needed on this tiny island.

There are several small shops in town where you can pick up limited grocery items, in Areora village, on the main road is the **ADC Store Ph. 33-028** where you will find a generous selection of local fruits and vegetables and limited food items. Over in Teenui Village stop and see Margaret Simpson at the **Vaiuroa Store**, she carries much the same selection as at the ADC Store for her neighbors in that village. If you are looking for some fresh bread try the **Akai Bakery Ph. 33-207** in the village of Mapumai. The shop is open daily from 10:00 AM on all but Saturday. Fresh bread disappears fast on Atiu, so it is always best to call Randy ahead of time to place your order. The bread pickup is after 10:00 AM when the bread is removed from the wood fired oven. Over in the village of Teenui, Joe and Hillary operate **"Jumbo Bakery" Ph. 33-181** where a variety of bread rolls, cheese rolls, scones and best of all, my favorite, doughnuts are made daily. If you can't make it to the bakery first thing in the morning, just go by the ADC Store where you can pick up some of Jumbo's baked goods later in the day. The other small shop is the **Centre Store Ph. 33-773** on the main road in Teenui Village, where locals congregate, sipping a cold drink, awaiting the Cook Islands Newspaper flown in daily from Rarotonga. They have plenty of cold beer, or so I am told.

Palmerston Island

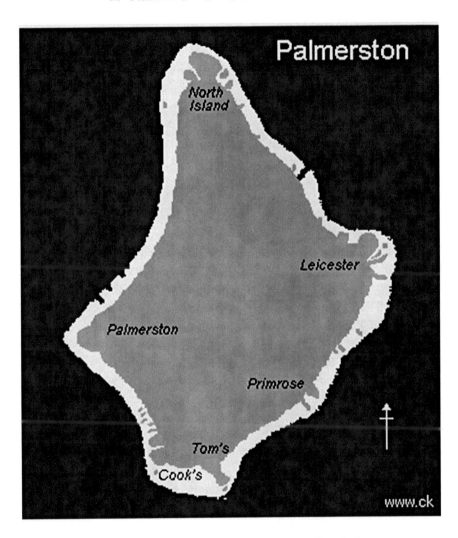

Palmerston is a speck on the map, approximately one square mile of land some 310 miles Northwest of Rarotonga. There are eight small *motus* (islets) that make up the island or atoll, with a border reef encircling the islets. The lagoon is large and about six to seven miles across. All of the islets are covered with coconut palms with the settlement on the island located on the northern part of the western islet.

A very long time ago, a wise man visited Polynesia, rounded him up three wives and picked an island on which to propagate. That island was Palmerston and that man was William Marsters. The year was 1862, when you could pretty much do as you wanted on a far-flung atoll. Today most of the residents of Palmerston are related to this "founding father" that built each of his three wives a home and started the ball rolling on Palmerston, so to speak. There are currently less than a hundred residents on the island, which isn't too bad when you consider the humble beginnings.

The current residents of Palmerston, less than 100 hardy souls, are mostly descendents of the original Marster's family. In recent times a number of Palmerston residents have married neighboring islanders. I would imagine if you ruled out sisters and cousins, you were left with pretty narrow pickings for potential spouses. If you acquired a bad reputation on the island, you would likely spend a lifetime alone.

Today Island Council, made up of community elders and an island mayor who addresses day-to-day matters, runs the island. The ancient driftwood church, damaged by hurricanes, has been replaced by a modern church building. While most homes have water catchment capabilities, there is a shared community catchment system with two large water tanks for those periods of drought. The island has a two-room school, but no teacher. Looking to get away from teaching in the big city? Contact the Palmerston Island Council for an application. Potential teachers will be happy to know that the island has electricity from 6 to 12, in both the morning and evening. Bring along plenty of VHS videos, television channels are somewhat limited. While limited in entertainment options, you will be rewarded with an unlimited supply of parrotfish fillets and all the coconuts you can eat.

The vast majority of the visitors to Palmerston are sailors making their way across French Polynesia on their way to Fiji. The island has a long tradition of welcoming cruising yachts, going back to the late 1950's. Word of the friendly residents of Palmerston has spread over the years. Many yachties contact the island on the marine band prior to leaving Aitutaki to find out if items are needed or mail needs to be delivered to the island. Over the years the locals have been so friendly that the yachting community goes out of their way to show their appreciation and return the favors. If you are aboard a yacht that will be calling on Palmerston please radio ahead from your last port at 1830 utc on 4038 mhz and enquire if there is anything you can bring along when you head out. Bring rice, flour, gasoline, and toys and games for the children, the islanders will appreciate it and your generosity will be returned in double.

Getting There

Much like a trip to neighboring Pukapuka, the term you can't get there from here comes to mind when considering a trip to tiny Palmerston Island. There is no scheduled airline service to Palmerston, which doesn't matter, as there is no airstrip located on the island. Island freighters do make infrequent stops on Palmerston on their way to Pukapuka from Rarotonga. Please read the section in the front of this book referring to Inter-Island freighters before considering this method of travel. The freighter service is unpredictable so it would be my suggestion that you visit only if you have a very open schedule and desire a real escape from society and our culture. Remember, no restaurants or bars, no supermarkets, no television or newspapers, but maybe that is exactly what you are looking for.

Getting Around

Where are you going?

Where To Stay

There are no commercial accommodations on Palmerston. Check with the Tourism Board, or local travel agents in Rarotonga, for the possibility of a home stay. As I have stated in this section on other remote islands, a home stay can be very rewarding. Your hosts will become your guides, your entertainment, historians and possibly your storytellers. It is also possible by the end of your stay that they may become some of your best friends. The only difficulty with a home stay is knowing how long you will be on the island, Cook Islander's are notoriously friendly, but if the freighter does not arrive for a couple of months, you may wear out even a Cook Islander's welcome and patience. Take along pencils, pens coloring books and old magazines, for these items are cherished by children of the out-islands and they will endear you to the parents as you explain that the freighter will not be here for another six weeks.

In recent years I have received many E-Mails from readers worldwide requesting more information about traveling to the more isolated islands of the Cook Islands. As stated elsewhere, travel is difficult and infrequent flights and freighters create havoc with schedules. That being said if you are intent upon visiting the likes of Rakahanga, Pukapuka, Nassau or Palmerston I would suggest you first contact either the Island Mayor or the Pastor of CICC Church on the island you wish to visit. I suppose it is a sign of our times that folks would like to escape civilization and visit remote islands. These two people are your best bet to try and find lodging possibilities amongst their fellow islanders. Palmerston *has* telephone service, but there are presently only four lines on the island. Two of these phones are pay phones; one is located inside the telecom building, while the second is outside the building. The outside phone **Ph. (682) 37-685** is available 24 hours a day and requires a Kia Orana calling card for all outgoing calls. The inside pay phone **Ph. (682) 37-684** is available only during normal business hours. In addition the Telecom Office has a fax line **Fax. (682) 37-683,** which is available during normal business hours. In case you wondered the fourth line is the Telecom office line. I would suggest sending a fax communication to either the mayor or pastor of the CICC church, or name both in the fax, the telecom office will likely pass on your communication, if you don't hear back in a reasonable time, you can attempt a phone call and have the party hailed. Another possible contact is a cellular listing for the **Palmerston Island Administration at (682) 54-660** as well as a couple of associated E-mail addresses, **palmerstonisland@hotmail.com** or **pamati@palmerstonisland.gov.ck** If you make the trip, good luck and be sure and pass along the information on to the author so that I can add the contacts to the next edition of this book.

Where To Eat

As stated above there are no restaurants on Palmerston, so you will be eating with your home stay family. You will want to bring along some major food supplies as well as bottled water and packaged snacks with you to Palmerston. You may wait for a freighter for a very long time on Palmerston, so canned meat and non-perishable food should be taken with you on the freighter. There is no baggage limit on the island freighter, so take what you feel you can't live without for a few months.

Suwarrow Atoll

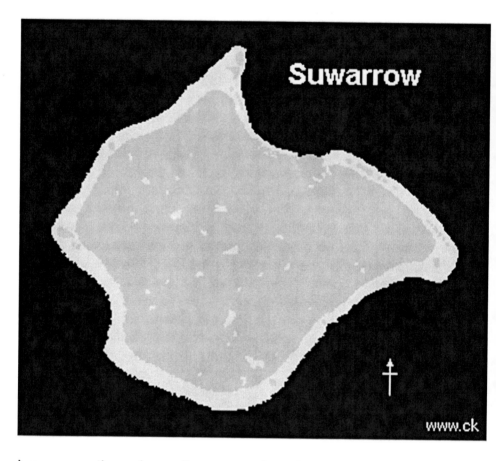

I suppose there is really no need to include Suwarrow in a guidebook on the Cook Islands, after all, there is any transportation to or place to stay on this tiny island. But the island itself has been a strange and mysterious place over the years. New Zealander Tom Neale lived alone on Suwarrow for many years and penned his classic, *An Island to Oneself*, which describes his time on the island and his desire for isolation. Robert Dean Frisbee described surviving a hurricane on Suwarrow by tying himself and others to a large tree, in his book

The Island of Desire. So over the years the island has maintained a mysterious presence in the literature of the region and Suwarrow is itself, the very image of that romantic South Seas Atoll that we all can picture in our minds.

Today Suwarrow is visited primarily by yachties on their way to and from Rarotonga, Bora Bora and Samoa. The lagoon offers shelter and the reef offers fresh fish to the sailor. The island is now officially a Marine Park. Caretakers live in Tom Neale's old house, guarding the fruit of the remaining coconut trees. The caretakers are living the life of isolation that Tom wrote about over fifty years ago; things haven't changed much in those fifty years or figure to change much in the next fifty year.

A Plea To Passing Yachties

The Suwarrow National Park Legislation was established in 1978. The island has a category IV status from the (IUCN) International Union for the Conservation for Natural. Today the legislative process for the preservation of this fragile marine and island environment is still under review. For the casual visitor to the park, the island and its environs offer many positive attractions. The allure of a safe haven, the opportunity to walk on dry land, the desire to drink fresh coconut water and the potential of meeting like minded travelers.

The clichés bestowing the 'healing properties' of the Cook Islands first national park fill the visitors log at the anchorage cove. There can be over 20 yachts at anchor at one time and up to 300 vessels visit the park during a single year. However, Suwarrow is not one of the three approved port-of-calls into the Cook Islands. A harsh reality for the Cook Islander's first national park is the flotsam, debris and litter that the passing parade of visitors has left behind. As a result, there is now a desperate need to clean the island of all this trash. The people of the Cook Islands ask all park visitors to take all litter and recyclable wastes away and allow larger environmental services to dispose of them in their more robust environments. Cook Islanders wish all visitors to the park a safe and pleasant stay, the future and well being of Suwarrow rests in your hands.

Pukapuka

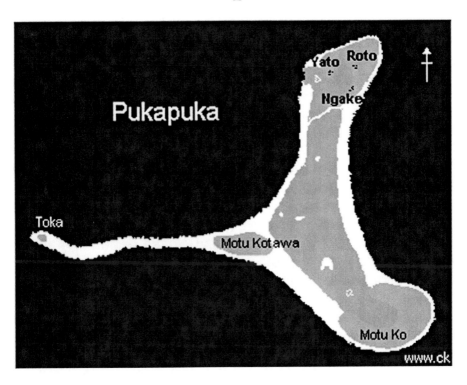

Cyclone Percy—the fourth of five cyclones that hit the Cook Islands over a five-week period in 2005—laid waste to most of Pukapuka and its lagoon. The hardy people that inhabit Pukapuka have shaken off the effects of the cyclone and continue to rebuild the houses on the island. After the cyclone the New Zealand Air Force flew over the island and reported that only ten percent of the islands homes survived intact. Makes you want to stop by, shake some hands and pitch in. My hat is off to those crazy Pukapukan's; hope to make it to your island someday.

It is said that the prettiest women in all of Polynesia live on Pukapuka, the island is also known as "the island of danger"

223

and American Robert Dean Frisbie described the island as "the island of desire" in his 1920's classic, The Book of Puka Puka. I wonder if pretty women, desire and danger are related? I'm afraid I don't have the answer to that question, but I will tell you that back in 1525 a tidal wave decimated the population of Pukapuka, killing all but 17 people—15 men and 2 women. These seventeen people, or should I say these lucky two women, were able to repopulate the island, so maybe there is some truth to the first sentence "and women, desire and danger are prevalent on Pukapuka."

"Danger Island", like many of the outer islands, is not an island at all, but an atoll that is made up of three small islets, connected by a barrier reef. The three islets are *Wale* (Pukapuka), *Motu* Ko and *Motu* Kotawa. The three main villages of *Yato (leeward)*, *Rotu* (central) and *Ngake* (windward) are all located on the main islet of Pukapuka, while the other two islets are used for crop production.

While Pukapuka is part of the Northern Group of the Cook Islands, it is geographically located far closer to Samoa than it is to Rarotonga. The island is 700 miles Northwest of Rarotonga, with tiny Palmerston Island, it's nearest neighbor, another 45 miles Northwest of Pukapuka. While English is the primary language in the Cook Islands, the three hundred people of Pukapuka speak a slightly different version of Maori, which is closer to Samoan than Cook Island Maori.

Pukapuka has a fairly abundant animal life; pigs, chicken and rats arrived with man. Sea birds are surprisingly scarce, apparently preferring neighboring Nassau and the uninhabited Suwarrow for there nesting spots. The local land cuckoo and pigeon are left, but near extinction. The island sports three kinds of butterflies, five kinds of dragonflies and plenty of those pesky mosquitoes. A wide variety of fish call the waters near and lagoon of Pukapuka their home. The island is blessed with three concrete cisterns, so fresh water is not a problem on Pukapuka. The land of Pukapuka is of sufficient quality to allow the cultivation of crops and a few of the lower swampy areas have been planted with taro and bananas. It is said that additional crops could be raised if population increases. Population was listed as 664 at the last census in 2001, but has decreased since that time, at least partly due to Cyclone Percy, but also caused by younger people migrating to Rarotonga and New Zealand.

If you are lucky enough to arrange for a visit to Pukapuka, you will benefit from a somewhat different perspective of Cook Island life. The island practices communal living, which means the work, food and profits equally distributed among the people of the three villages. You will enjoy a simple, unpretentious lifestyle, the legendary friendship of the Cook Islanders, with the bonus of customs and traditions of Samoa.

Getting There

You have heard the term you can't get there from here? Well this is nearly the case in Pukapuka. There is no scheduled airline service to Pukapuka, but there is an airstrip located on the island. You can contact Air Rarotonga Ph. 22-888 in Rarotonga but I doubt if they will have any scheduled service unless they have a charter headed that way. Keep in mind that you will be limited to 16 kilograms (33.2 Lbs.) of checked luggage on your flight, which will limit what you can take along for what will likely be a lengthy stay on the island. Island freighters do make occasional trips to Pukapuka from Rarotonga; please read the section in the front of this book referring to Inter-Island freighters before considering this method of travel. The freighter service is unpredictable so it would be my suggestion that you visit only if you have a very open schedule and desire a real escape from society and our culture. Remember, no restaurants or bars, no supermarkets, no television or newspapers, but maybe that is exactly what you are looking for?

Getting Around

I have used the term, "hoof it", far too many times when telling my fellow traveler the mode of transportation on various out islands. Since Pukapuka has little that one could call a road, you will travel between the three villages on foot. You need not worry about the coral *makatea* that is prevalent in the Southern Group Islands, so enjoy your walk in your flip-flops

.

Where To Stay

There are no commercial accommodations on Pukapuka. Check with the Tourism Board, or local travel agents in Rarotonga, for the possibility of a home stay. A home stay can be very rewarding; your hosts will become your guides, your entertainment, historians and possibly your storytellers. It is also possible by the end of your stay that they may become some of your best friends. The only difficulty with a home stay is knowing how long you will be on the island, Cook Islander's are notoriously friendly, but if the freighter does not arrive for a couple of months, you may wear out even a Cook Islander's welcome and patience.

In recent years I have received many E-Mails from readers worldwide requesting more information about traveling to the more isolated islands of the Cook Islands. As stated elsewhere, travel is difficult and infrequent flights and freighters create havoc with schedules. That being said if you are intent upon visiting the likes of Rakahanga, Pukapuka, Nassau or

Palmerston I would suggest you first contact either the Island Secretary or the Pastor of CICC Church on the island you wish to visit. I suppose it is a sign of our times that folks would like to escape civilization and visit remote islands. These two people are your best bet to try and find lodging possibilities amongst their fellow islanders. The island secretary on Pukapuka can be reached at (682) 41-712 and the CICC Pastor can be reached at (682) 41-023 and no they don't have E-Mail. If you make the trip, good luck and be sure and pass along the information on to the author so that I can add the contacts to the next edition of this book.

Where To Eat

As stated above there are no restaurants on Pukapuka, so you will be eating with your home stay family. You will want to bring along some major food supplies as well as bottled water and packaged snacks with you to Pukapuka. You may wait for a freighter for a very long time on these outer islands, so canned meat and non-perishable food should be taken with you. There is no baggage limit on the island freighter, so take what you feel you can't live without for a few months.

Nassau Island

This island could be termed a distant suburb of Pukapuka, which lies about fifty miles northwest of Nassau. It seems that Europeans, after having tried for years to run a coconut plantation on the island, sold the island in 1945 to the government of the Cook Islands for a paltry NZ$2500.00. The government in turn sold the island back to the Pukapukans in 1951 for the same sum, and the island chiefs on Pukapuka have been smiling ever since. They have become South Seas land barons and picked up some prime *taro* fields for future generations as a bonus. Stay tuned for future development plans on Nassau.

Nassau is a true island, unlike the other northern group islands, which are in reality atolls. For those of you who must know these things, the island was named after an American whaling ship that called on the island back in 1835. There are less than 100 semi-permanent residents of the island. I term them semi-permanent residents because I have been told come July of each year they all leave for Pukapuka and Rarotonga for the Constitution Celebrations, returning two months later well rested and with immense knowledge of the constitution or vast knowledge of celebrations, I'm not sure which. While this is an interesting story, I find it hard to believe that the island remains deserted for these two months. To investigate this story I am enlisting volunteers to travel to Nassau in late July and report back with the true story of Nassau. You should have no problem finding a place to stay during this trip.

Nassau was severely damaged by Cyclone Percy in February of 2005. With kind aid from New Zealand, the infrastructure of the island was restored in October of that same year. Major repairs were needed to the health clinic, power station and Island

Council meeting house. In addition a completely new school was built.

Getting There

If you are visiting Nassau you will need to be patient and persistent, for there is no regularly scheduled transportation to or from the island and no organized accommodations on the island. You could fly to Pukapuka, but that island has no regularly scheduled service from Rarotonga. The inter-island freighter does call on Nassau, but you will most likely take the freighter to Pukapuka and then hire a captain to take you the last fifty miles to Nassau. See the section on inter-island travel at the front of this book for information on the joy of freighter travel in the Cook Islands.

Getting Around

The only village on Nassau is on the north side of the island and the only way to get around the island is to follow the paths that lead to the *taro* swamps and coconut groves. You can circle the mile-long oval island on the beach in about an hour.

Things To Do

You won't be watching television and the Cook Island phone book shows no listings for Nassau, so you wont be talking on the phone. The only permanent link to the outside world is a satellite earth station established by engineers from Telecom Cook Islands. Regular telephone service was planned to start in 2004, but Cyclone Percy and delays have backed that date up, hopefully service will be established in the near future. For now, the island can be reached by high-frequency radio link. Contact Telecom Cook Islands at 020 to arrange a call.

You will be situated on a very small island in the South Pacific and chances are you can snorkel, swim and fish to your heart's content. Make friends with the locals and they will take you fishing in their canoes.

One unique thing to do on Nassau is to wander on down to the *Manuvai* and check out the shipwreck. It seems the ship ran into the island on one clear, calm night back in 1988, when the boat, in ideal conditions made far better time than it's captain anticipated and well, ran smack dab into Nassau under a full head of steam. I heard the story from Don Silk, half of the legendary Boyd and Silk Shipping Company founders, one night at Trader Jack's. The story still brings tears to his eyes and surely put a dent in his wallet. The wreck is a very prominent feature on Nassau and will be for the next hundred years; a testimonial to the fact that somebody needs to stand watch at all times.

Where To Stay

There are no organized accommodations presently on Nassau. The only accommodations would have to be a home stay. Talk to the tourist board in Avarua before you leave Rarotonga, they may have some names or you can talk to the various pastors of churches if you arrive on Nassau without accommodation. Nobody will stay homeless long with the generosity of these islanders, but keep in mind there limited resources. The Island Council governs Nassau over on its neighbor Pukapuka, if you are interested in a home stay talk to the Pukapuka Island Council at (682) 41-034.

Where To Eat

There are no places to eat on Nassau, but I will assume you have made some arrangements to stay with someone on the island. You will need to bring along much of your own food, as the island has limited resources. The copra harvesters imported pigs and chickens onto the island and their descendents are still around the island. Bananas and taro is grown on the island, along with a limited amount of vegetables. There are a variety of fish to be caught in the sea around the island, so bring along a fishing pole to help with the food supply.

Rakahanga

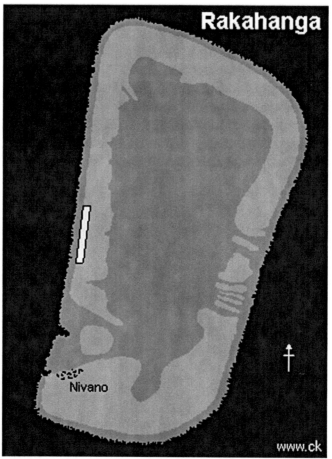

A trip to Rakahanga makes Manihiki seem like a busy place. There are less than 200 people on the island, which has a smaller lagoon than Manihiki. The only settlement on the island is Matara, which is located at the southwest opening in the reef. The soil on Rakahanga is far superior to its neighbor Manihiki, so the locals grow breadfruit and taro and other crops to sell on that island. The only other export crop is *copra*, the meat or fiber of dried coconut, which is used to flavor products, in recent years this market has dwindled, as they probably can produce

an artificial flavor a lot cheaper, so don't count on becoming a copra baron on Rakahanga.

My visit to Rakahanga coincided with a visit by Hurricane Divi and both the island and myself sustained damage as a result of the hurricane. I elected to stay on the island freighter *Manu Nui* as the ship was unloaded, but word of my visit had reached the island and a host of islanders came out on the barge to meet, "Papa Mike" and tell me of life on Rakahanga. I enjoyed visiting with the teenage islanders, who wanted to know if I knew Michael Jackson or Jennifer Lopez. It seems that the New Zealand issues of *People* magazine were making the rounds even as far as the Northern Cook Islands and I as an American from California, was

expected to be close friends with all these stars. It didn't help that my last name was Hollywood. The pictures of Rakahanga featured in this section, show the beauty of the lagoon and simple life of the islanders know wonder they are so friendly.

Phone service was completed shortly prior to our arrival on the island and the Rakahangans were quite proud of their new link with the outside world.

Getting There

Unless you are traveling by yacht or inter island freighter, you will most likely arrive on Rakahanga by taking a boat ride from neighboring Manihiki. To find a skipper, talk to locals on Manihiki or ask at your accommodation, they will know of someone who can take you the thirty miles to Rakahanga. As this book is being written work has begun on a small ferry that will be used to provide transportation between Rakahanga and Manihiki, once this ferry is in service there will be regularly scheduled service between the two islands. Island freighters stop at Rakahanga after leaving Manihiki and this is a possible transportation alternative from Rarotonga, please read the section in the front of this book referring to Inter-Island freighters before considering this method of travel. Airfare to neighboring Manihiki is substantial and freighter service is unpredictable, so travel to Rakahanga only if you have a very open schedule and desire a real escape from society and our culture. Remember, no restaurants or bars, no markets, no television or newspapers, but maybe that is exactly what you are looking for.

Getting Around

There is no public transportation on Rakahanga, so the only alternative is to hoof it. There is only one main village on Rakahanga so what limited services exist on the island, are accessible by walking.

Things To Do

You most likely will be staying with locals and you should plan on helping with their sustenance farming or lending a hand with the fishing. They will show you the lagoon and teach you how to climb a coconut tree. Take along a bunch of novels and read or perhaps write your great novel. In general you will find it hard to spend your money. There is a small store on the island, but supplies are meager and the island freighter arrives infrequently, so often there is little to buy. Enjoy each day and enjoy the life of a true beachcomber.

Places To Stay

There are no organized accommodations on Rakahanga, though I was told there were a few simple concrete block structures that could be rented if one was willing to live with a floor of sand. The only other accommodations would have to be a home stay One thing is for sure, nobody will stay homeless long with the generosity of these islanders, but keep in mind there limited resources.

In recent years I have received many E-Mails from readers worldwide requesting more information about traveling to the more isolated islands of the Cook Islands. As stated elsewhere, travel is difficult and infrequent freighters create havoc with schedules. That being said if you are intent upon visiting Rakahanga, I would suggest you first contact either the Island Administration **Ph. (682) 44-036** or the Pastor of CICC Church **Ph. (682) 44-000**. Have a great stay.

Where To Eat

Well they shut down the drive thru at Burger King and the Outback Steakhouse was destroyed in the last hurricane. Whatever you are going to eat I hope you brought it with you because Rakahanga has no restaurants. Hopefully you have not arrived without food. Canned goods and snacks are best brought along if you came by freighter or arrived by sail on a visiting yacht. The locals will share but their food sources are limited. If you arranged for a home stay, the food question will have been discussed and arrangements made, you may be able to buy light snacks at a shop in the village. Locals prepare a dried and salted tuna jerky that they will share with you. Refrigeration is a luxury in the out-islands so most everything is eaten fresh or dried for later consumption. The local fruit is excellent and you certainly won't starve on the island.

Part 3

Reference

Bibliography

There are a number of books that I would suggest you read about the Cook Islands, listed below are many of my favorites. It is not a complete list but represents the books on and about the region that I found interesting and entertaining.

Cook Islands Companion
Elliot Smith
Pacific Publishing Company

Although Elliot's book was last published back in 1994, it still has a lot of cultural, and historical information that is timeless. The book is not available from the publisher, but used copies are available at Amazon.com.

Rarotonga & The Cook Islands
Nancy Keller & Errol Hunt
Lonely Planet Publications

Australia's mass-market guidebook publisher has recently published their fifth edition of the Cook Islands book. As always, there books are long on facts and a bit dry to the reader, so you are the judge.

South Pacific Handbook
David Stanley
Moon Travel Handbooks

David's book is recommended for those who wish to travel beyond the Cook Islands and explore the entire South Pacific. There is a section in his handbook about Rarotonga and the Cook Islands and the book has detailed maps of both

Rarotonga and Avarua. It is a good companion to the book you are reading and the Canadian author has been writing about the South Pacific for over forty years. Visit David's Website at www.southpacific.org for a wealth of information on the entire South Pacific region.

How To Get Lost & Found In The Cook Islands
John Mc Dermott
Waikiki Publishing Company

This book is a classic. Originally published in 1979 for Air New Zealand, the book details the travels of the author and his "lady navigator" wife, who visited the Cook Islands in the late seventies. The photo on the back cover is worth whatever you have to pay for a used copy. Try for a used copy from Amazon.com or other used bookstores.

Tales Of The South Pacific
James W. Michener
Mass Market Paperback

There are plenty of used copies around of this classic novel set in the South Pacific. Relax on the beach and read one of Michener's best and the basis for the movie and play of the same name.

Vaka (Polynesian Canoe)
Dr. Tom Davis
Institute Of Pacific Studies

The former Prime Minister of the Cook Islands wrote the novel Vaka about the historical migration of the Polynesian people back in 1992. In addition to the novel Dr. Davis wrote, Doctor To The Islands, about his life prior to entering politics and an autobiography titled, Island Boy. I had the pleasure of meeting Dr. Davis on my trip to the Cook's in 2003, sitting on the stool at

Trader Jack's, he was as sharp as a tack and very much aware of worldwide politics. His passing will be missed by many Worldwide, but mostly by his countrymen in the Cook Islands.

From Kauri Trees To Sunlit Seas
Don Silk
Ashford Press

This hard to find classic tells the tale of Silk & Boyd Shipping and the trials and tribulations of running a shoestring shipping business in the South Pacific. The tales of shipwrecks, bureaucrats and political snafus is entertaining to anyone who enjoys a good tale. Stop by Trader Jack's at happy hour and you may very well bump into Don or his partner Bud Boyd, last I checked Jack still had a few copies of the book for sale at the restaurant. You may be able to pick up a copy of this or other books suggested in this section at Bounty Bookstore in Avarua.

An Island To Oneself
Tom Neale
Collins, London

Tom is the famous hermit of Suwarrow and his book of his six years on the island. The book is kind of a Cook Island's Robinson Crusoe story. I don't know where you can find the book, but if you have some patience, you can read the book on a Website, visit Taori's Pacific Island Site, www.tvds.net/ and click on the link to the book.

The Book Of Puka Puka
Robert Dean Frisbie
Mutual Publishing Company

This book of short stories was written back in 1928 and last published in 1957, so as you can guess it is hard to find a copy. Mr. Frisbie was an American that moved to the island of

Pukapuka and at the time was the only foreigner on the island. He learned the language, married a local woman and wrote about it in his book. In his follow up book, Island Of Desire, he describes the tale of lashing his children to mahogany trees during the hurricane of 1942.

The Cook Islands
Ewan Smith
Island Image, Rarotonga

If you visit the islands and want to take back dazzling images of Rarotonga and the Cook Islands, this is the book for you. The photos are outstanding and this book will show nicely on your coffee table. The only drawback is you will have to explain where the islands are located, as few know what we have discovered

.
The Cook Islands Natural Heritage Project has a field guide on mountain tracks and plants and there are several other brochures on Rarotonga that can be picked up at The Bounty Bookstore, next to the Post Office in Avarua. Ask at the counter and they can direct you to a section that offers books of local interest. Some books are also available at the Cook Islands Trading Company (CITC) store on the main road in Avarua.

The list above is a short list, but I think it represents the books most likely to be of interest to the visitor. Copies of the book listed and many others are available at Rarotonga's Library & Museum Society Ph. 20-725 and the National Library. Visitors can sign up for a temporary borrowers card, by paying a refundable deposit and a small fee. The Museum and Library are both located on the outskirts of Avarua; turn inland at the Paradise Inn. Call as to the hours that they are open.

About the Author

In January of 2003 Mike Hollywood spent two months living and traveling in the Cook Islands, surviving a cyclone (hurricane) on his inter-island steamship trip to the Northern Group Islands. He has since returned to the islands in 2004 and 2008 to research this second edition of **Papa Mike's Cook Islands Handbook.** Besides the Cook Islands Handbook, Papa Mike has published, **Papa Mike's Palau Islands Handbook** in 2005 and **The West Indies on $50.00 A Day**, in 2000. Mike resides in Emigrant, Montana (during the summer).

Contact the author at:
Post Office Box 21
Emigrant, MT 59027
E-mail: bimbolimbotravel@aol.com
Website: www.mikehollywood.com

Index

Accommodations 5, 10, 16, 24, 28, 29, 33, 35, 40, 77, 78, 80,
    81, 85, 99, 112, 116, 136, 137, 143, 154, 160, 167, 169, 171,
    172, 179, 201, 206, 219, 227, 230, 231, 236
Airports 10, 11, 16, 23, 47, 52, 79, 90, 91, 99, 100, 102, 111,
    112, 113, 115, 116, 118, 119, 126, 136, 137, 139, 140, 141,
    146, 154, 170, 171, 191, 204, 207, 209, 212
Aitutaki .. 3, 13, 26, 28, 29, 31, 35, 36, 37, 38, 53, 54, 61, 62, 69,
    134, 135, 136, 137, 139, 140, 141, 142, 143, 144, 145, 146,
    148, 149, 150, 152, 153, 154, 155, 160, 161, 164, 206, 218
    Getting Around 137
    Getting There 136
    Places To Stay 143
    Things To Do.. 138
    Where To Eat 160
Aitutaki Pearl Beach Resort 144
Ara Moana Bungalows... 168, 169
Are Manuiri Guesthouse 209
Are Renga Motel.. 49, 50, 117
Are Tamanu Beach Hotel.. 148
Ariana Bungalows 50, 117
Aroa's Beachside Inn 49, 93
Aroko Bungalows.. 49, 50, 101, 102
Atiu.2, 29, 38, 137, 180, 190, 203, 204, 205, 206, 207, 208, 209,
    210, 211, 212, 213
    Getting Around 206
    Getting There 205
    Places To Stay 209
    Things To Do.. 206
    Where To Eat 213
Atiu Villas 208, 210, 213
Atupa Orchid Units.. 118

Avarua . 10, 11, 12, 14, 16, 18, 19, 48, 52, 53, 59, 63, 67, 68, 74,
    75, 76, 77, 84, 97, 98, 99, 102, 110, 111, 114, 118, 123, 126,
    132, 179, 201, 204, 231, 240, 241, 242
Babe's Place... 168, 169, 170
Banks... 10, 11, 21
Bars 111, 132, 133, 144, 218, 227, 235
Beachcomber Gallery 75
Books.................... 32, 42, 67, 113, 219, 239, 241, 242
Bus Schedule Rarotonga... 49
Castawa Beach Villas.. 100
Club Raro 49, 50, 96, 97
Cost Of Trip 6
Courtesies & Dress... 20
Crime.. 20
Crown Beach Resort 49, 50, 58, 82, 102, 126
Departure Tax... 102
Drivers Licence.. 12
Edgewater Resort................... 49, 50, 56, 57, 84
Electric Service.. 11, 12
Entry Requirements 5, 9
Fishing . 62, 63, 82, 133, 135, 142, 164, 168, 175, 176, 177, 183,
    192, 193, 197, 200, 207, 208, 231, 232, 236
Flight Schedule Air Rarotonga................................ 29
Food .. 5, 6, 16, 32, 33, 40, 42, 43, 54, 64, 76, 84, 123, 126, 127,
    128, 162, 171, 172, 173, 184, 190, 192, 194, 220, 226, 228,
    232, 236, 237
General Information.. 5, 9
Getting There. 136, 137, 167, 176, 181, 191, 199, 205, 218, 226,
    230, 235
Gina's Garden Lodges... 153
Health 18, 41, 66, 74
Hiking... 65, 67, 167
Horseback Riding 74
How To Use This Guidebook....................................... 5
Inter Island Travel.. 29
Internet 14, 25, 27, 97, 115

Introduction 7, 20
Island Nights 54, 55, 161
Island Sea Cruises...63
Kia Orana Guesthouse 212
Kii Kii Motel 113
Kopeka Lodge...211, 212
Lagoon Lodges 49, 51, 89, 90, 92
Little Polynesian.......................... 49, 51, 97, 98
Mail Service 19
Maina Sunset Resort 149
Manahiki.............. 29, 35, 38, 74, 174, 176, 177, 179, 233, 235
   Getting Around 176
   Getting There 176
   Places To Stay 177
   Things To Do..176
   Where To Eat 179
Manahiki Guesthouse 178
Manahiki Lagoon Lookout..............................178
Manea Beach Villas 94
Mangaia 29, 38, 165, 166, 167, 168, 169, 170, 171, 172, 181, 190
   Getting Around 167
   Getting There 167
   Places To Stay 168
   Things To Do..168
   Where To Eat 172
Mangaia Lodge 169, 171
Manuia Beach Resort 102
Mauke 18, 29, 38, 180, 181, 182, 183, 184, 185, 188, 205
   Getting Around 182
   Getting There 181
   Places To Stay 185
   Things To Do..182
   Where To Eat 188
Mauke Cove Lodge...183

Mitiaro 29, 38, 180, 181, 189, 190, 191, 192, 193, 194, 195, 196, 205

    Getting Around 191

    Getting There 191

    Places To Stay 193

    Things To Do 191

    Where To Eat 196

Moana Sands Hotel & Villas 95

Muri Beachcomber 49, 50, 96

Nassau Island 229

Newspapers 22, 218, 227, 235

Nukaroa Beach Guesthouse 194, 195

Pacific Computers 12

Pacific Resort 49, 50, 57, 80, 81, 133, 145, 146, 152

Pacific Resort—Aitutaki 145

Palm Grove Hotel 91

Palmerston Island 216, 218, 225

Paradise Cove Guesthouse 154

Paradise Inn 49, 50, 110, 133, 242

Paratrooper Motel 154

Penrhyn 12, 29, 35, 38, 40, 41, 74, 197, 198, 199, 200, 201

    Getting Around 199

    Getting There 199

    Places To Stay 200

    Things To Do 199

    Where To Eat 201

Picture Taking 21

Planning Your Trip 6, 25, 36, 145

Puaikura Reef Lodges 51, 99

Pukapuka 39, 40, 218, 224, 225, 226, 227, 228, 229, 230, 242

Rakahanga 12, 40, 74, 175, 233, 234, 235, 236

Ranginui's Retreat 150

Rarotonga 5, 6, 7, 9, 10, 11, 13, 16, 21, 22, 23, 24, 25, 26, 27, 28, 29, 31, 32, 33, 35, 36, 37, 38, 40, 41, 46, 47, 48, 52, 53, 54, 55, 60, 62, 65, 66, 67, 68, 69, 70, 72, 73, 74, 77, 79, 80, 81, 82, 84, 85, 89, 91, 93, 94, 95, 96, 97, 98, 99, 100, 101,

102, 103, 104, 110, 111, 112, 113, 114, 116, 117, 118, 125, 126, 131, 135, 136, 137, 141, 143, 144, 149, 160, 165, 167, 173, 176, 177, 178, 179, 181, 182, 190, 191, 198, 199, 200, 201, 204, 205, 206, 216, 218, 219, 222, 225, 226, 227, 229, 230, 231, 235, 239, 240, 242
Getting Around 219, 227, 230, 235
Getting There 218, 226, 230, 235
Places To Stay 219, 227, 231, 236
Thing To Do... 230, 235
Where To Eat 220, 228, 232, 236
Rarotonga Backpackers... 114
Rarotonga Beach Bungalows... 103, 104
Rarotongan Beach Resort 56, 57, 75, 81, 90, 144
Rarotongan Sunset 49, 50, 98
Reefwalking 64
Restaurants... 21, 23, 77, 84, 85, 94, 96, 98, 101, 102, 103, 110, 111, 112, 113, 127, 139, 144, 151, 160, 179, 201, 218, 220, 227, 228, 235, 236
Aitutaki... 160
Rino's Beach Bungalows 152
Scuba & Snorkeling 58
Seabreeze Lodge... 193
Shopping... 21, 53, 74, 76, 110
Soa's Guesthouse... 200
Sokala Villas 49, 50, 85, 101
Sunday.... 21, 22, 26, 29, 38, 57, 68, 76, 98, 100, 123, 131, 161, 184, 193, 199
Sunny Beach Lodge... 152, 153
Surfing 67, 68
Suwarrow Atoll 221
Taparere Lodge 211
Taxes 15
Telephone 13
Tiao Shipping Ltd. 39, 136
Tiare Bungalows 177
Tiare Holiday Cottages 185

Tiare Village.. 49, 111
Time..... 10, 13, 18, 19, 22, 26, 27, 28, 29, 31, 32, 33, 37, 38, 39,
    44, 47, 49, 62, 63, 64, 69, 72, 74, 77, 79, 93, 102, 133, 136,
    138, 140, 141, 143, 145, 149, 167, 169, 170, 171, 172, 175,
    176, 177, 193, 198, 199, 200, 205, 206, 208, 211, 217, 220,
    221, 228, 231, 242
Tipping.. 16
Tourism...........................7, 8, 23, 154, 177, 192, 219, 227
Tours ...23, 27, 29, 35, 47, 60, 62, 67, 69, 70, 72, 73, 82, 84, 91,
    92, 96, 101, 119, 136, 137, 145, 149, 152, 154, 166, 168,
    170, 171, 175, 176, 178, 192, 195, 206, 207, 209
Trader Jacks.. 132
Travel To The Outer Islands 29, 36
TV & Radio 23
Vaikoa Units 155
Vara's Beach House............................. 49, 51, 96, 116
Visas.. 11
Visitors Permits.. 10
Water...7, 17, 40, 44, 59, 61, 63, 65, 66, 82, 92, 94, 96, 97, 101,
    113, 139, 140, 145, 171, 172, 175, 177, 178, 183, 191, 200,
    207, 212, 220, 228
Whale Watching 68
What You Need For Trip....................................... 30